DIALOGUES ON FUNDAMENTAL QUESTIONS OF SCIENCE AND PHILOSOPHY

Dialogues
On Fundamental Questions of
Science and Philosophy

BY

A. Pfeiffer

Translated from the German
by Jutta Mendelssohn and Ursula Meadows

With a Foreword by Kurt Mendelssohn, F.R.S.

PERGAMON PRESS LIMITED

OXFORD · LONDON · EDINBURGH · NEW YORK
TORONTO · SYDNEY · PARIS · BRAUNSCHWEIG

Pergamon Press Ltd., Headington Hill Hall, Oxford
4 & 5 Fitzroy Square, London W.1
Pergamon Press (Scotland) Ltd., 2 & 3 Teviot Place, Edinburgh 1
Pergamon Press Inc., 44—01 21st Street, Long Island City, New York 11101
Pergamon of Canada, Ltd., 6 Adelaide Street East, Toronto, Ontario
Pergamon Press (Aust.) Pty. Ltd., 20—22 Margaret Street, Sydney, New South Wales
Pergamon Press S.A.R.L., 24 rue des Écoles, Paris 5e
Vieweg & Sohn GmbH, Burgplatz 1, Braunschweig

IN MEMORY OF MY TEACHERS
WALTER NERNST AND MAX PLANCK

CONTENTS

A Foreword by Kurt Mendelssohn, F.R.S. XI

Introduction

First dialogue (introducing the range of problems to be dealt with): 3

Science and philosophy — ideal values — scepticism and mysticism — biology and ethics — does an objective reality exist? — from quantum physics to religion — nature religions — science and superstition — religion and politics — science and art in place of religion.

First Part

Science and Theory of Cognition

Second dialogue (the philosophical problems of quantum physics): 13

Do elementary particles exist objectively? — Kant and the positivists — the philosopher as guardian of the physicist — the correspondence principle — individuality and objective existence — the wave of probability — uncertainty relation and errors in measurement — experimental conditions and results — the causality principle as a criterion of reality — two versions of the causality principle — chance and determinacy — the islands of interactions — free will and the causality principle.

Third dialogue (the theory of cognition of philosophic idealism and the starting point of philosophy): 28

Kant's circle syllogism — the positivistic fundamental conceptions — Fichte and Hegel — solipsism — philosophy and practice — the "physical" positivism — philosophy without assumptions? — Descartes' circle syllogism — deductive and inductive methods in natural science and philosophy — mathematics as science of experience — philosophy and individual sciences.

Fourth dialogue (the model theory of cognition): 36

Theory of cognition and psychology — theory of cognition and history of the development of species — learning as fundamental phenomenon of life — Pavlov's conditioned reflexes and perception — Haeckel's fundamental biogenetic law and the development of the ability of cognition — the mate-realistic theory of cognition — incessorial and excessorial creatures — of the infantilism of the "critical" philosophy — "matter" and "mind" or "spirit" — the natural "law" — materialism and pantheism — metaphysics of the will?

Second Part

The Ethical Problem — Nature and Culture

Fifth dialogue (ethical fundamental questions): 49

Ethics and natural science — ethics and practice — the urge for "good" and the categorical imperative — reason and inclination — moral and religion — culture and ethics — the decline of ethics — is religion necessary for the foundation of ethics? — Kant's religious postulates — the reward motive — the urge for self-preservation and reproduction — culture and biological viability — is culture inherently irrational? — the ethical conflict.

Sixth dialogue (on natural structures): 57

Destruction, annihilation, the struggle for existence — the concept of tension in inorganic and organic nature — internal tensions — reversible and irreversible processes — the inner harmony of natural structures — species concept and the individual — species concept as "idea" — animate beings as complex regulator — species concept as control programme — the concept of "good" and the concept of "species homo sapiens" — do ideas of the mind only exist?

Seventh dialogue (of the individual development and of the behaviour of animals): 66

Species concept of the structure of the body and species concept of the mode of life — structure of conduct of life — species concept and prototype of the individual development — prototype and environment — reflexes and instincts — learning and consciousness — goal-orientated instincts — complexes of characteristics as impulse release — the conflict of instincts — the influence of the animal on his environment — the prototype of the herd — obedience and disobedience of the domesticated animal — the mixed herd.

Eighth dialogue (ethics and culture): 83

Behaviour according to maxims — instinct and reason — love and sexuality — motherlove — the exploratory drive — ambition — the roots of culture — language — culture as result of a "feed-back" — the inner logic of the development of culture — structure of production, structure of society and system of values — individuality and egoism — the ethical primacy of society — the reasons for the decay of ethics — social consciousness and tradition of concepts.

Ninth dialogue (on the evaluation of single impulses and the relation between the individual and society): 101

"Eternal" virtues — sexual instinct and religion — biological standards of value? — the conscience — moral personal responsibility — concept of honour — professional or class-bound honour — the exploiting class as upholders of civilisation — on the moral reaction of the individual on society — the genius — the humanitarian ideal — ethics and negation of life — "inwardness" — the reasons for the social impotence of Christianity and the historical limitation of Christian ethics — active Christianity — does progress exist? — politics, economy and ethics.

Tenth dialogue (on the total conception of the ethical ideals): 116

Again the conflict of ethics — the Jesuitic casuistry — "optimum" and "least evil" — the integral assessment of the moral personality — esoteric solution of the ethical problem? — "mundus vult decipi" — theoretical insight and practical decision — the complex character of ethical ideas — the good and bad example for others — man is good — the fear of death — the philosopher as comforter — man as tool.

FOREWORD

Professor Pfeiffer's book is a document of his generation. He was born fourteen years before the outbreak of the First World War in a provincial German town. The atmosphere of law, order and stability of his early environment was further emphasized by the fact that his father was an attorney and Pfeiffer's fondness of concise if mildly legalistic argument clearly stems from this source. It already had become a habit with him when we first met in the late twenties at the Physics Department of Berlin University. This was the Berlin of the Threepenny Opera where standards of decency were sold as readily as the flesh and bogus shares. The world of his childhood had disappeared for ever.

Pfeiffer was neither corrupted nor did he become a moralist, but the ease with which man could be corrupted fascinated him and was observed by him with almost clinical detachment. However, Berlin at that time also had the largest concentration of Nobel Prize Laureates who laid the foundations of modern physics. The concepts of relativity and quantum mechanics were as far removed from classical physics as the morality of post-war Berlin from the tenets of Pfeiffer's childhood. As his book shows, he was profoundly impressed by this revolution in scientific thought but again he remained a spectator. He took an active part in our unending speculations on the meaning of these new concepts but chose for his work the safe and precise field of the theory of physical instruments.

Pfeiffer became chief scientist to a large instrument firm with which he stayed throughout the Nazi time and the war. Like many other German scientists who found themselves engulfed by the Russian advance, he spent a number of years in the Soviet Union. After his return he did not migrate to West Germany, a step which at that time only involved a twopenny ride on the Berlin Underground, but preferred to stay and work in the East. He is now Professor at an East German university.

The form which he has chosen for setting out his thoughts is that of a disputation in a manner similar to that employed by Galileo and many of his contemporaries. It requires little imagination to realise that it is a dialogue between Pfeiffer as a young man and Pfeiffer after he returned from Russia. The inherited and morally impeccable standards of B are set against the cool and merciless arguments of A, the man whose original concepts have been changed out of all recognition by the experience of life. What makes this book so interesting for us is that his experience of life has been different from our own.

Oxford, June 1966   *K. Mendelssohn*

INTRODUCTION

First Dialogue

In this, A poses science the task of conceiving uniform criteria for animate and inanimate nature as well as human society, and for man's striving for ideal values. He is convinced that reality can be recognised objectively, but not that there is, of necessity, a conflict between science and faith. He condemns the use of religion as a political means. He thinks that science and art are qualified to take the place of religion.

His partner, B, is disturbed by certain results of modern quantum physics which appear to him to have shaken the concept of the "objective truth". His scepticism is coupled with a certain mysticism. He cannot think that the realm of ideal values can be constructed on the basis of natural science only without the help of metaphysical concepts. He sees no way of bridging the gulf between the biological approach and the moral approach.

A Well, you have listened to our argument. Do you agree with my opinion?

B I was particularly interested in one of your statements. You claim that the rigorous, scientific contemplation of nature could be capable *only* of leading to a self-contained philosophy, and an absolutely positive philosophy at that. You even hinted that it could not help but lead to such a philosophy.

 I am bound to say that I cannot agree with this opinion unreservedly. After all, physics is becoming more and more the basic science of the natural sciences. The statements of physics, however, are increasingly taking on a decidedly mathematical character. I do not believe, for instance, that Maxwell's equations . . .

A . . . or Heisenberg's uncertainty relation or Schrodinger's wave equations. . .

B Exactly — I can see you understand what I mean. I think, therefore, it is hardly possible that one can start from knowledge of this kind and find a way to the realm of those values which it is the task of philosophy to open up. I simply cannot imagine how one could arrive, with this as a basis, at any positive statements about "good" and "evil", or about beauty or about truth. It appears to me, on the contrary, that precisely the most recent findings of physics make, for example, the concept of truth even more doubtful than it was in any case.

A Your remark shows that you incline to a general scepticism — we certainly do not agree if that is the case.

B I do not think you really understand what I mean to say. I am not at all a follower of an absolute scepticism. For instance, if I prepare a publication or write a report for which I get paid even, then I have certainly the conviction that what I state is correct and true — at least according to the generally used yardstick for truth and accuracy. If I did not believe that, I would be a swindler. But that was not really what I intended to say. I wanted rather to agree with Hamlet's opinion that there are more things in heaven and earth than our book learning . . .

A "— . . . than are dreamt of in our philosophy". To express it less gently than Shakespeare, that things exist which cannot be explained by strict science.

B Exactly. That is my considered opinion.

A You will not take it ill, will you, if I now accuse you of an inclination to mysticism which I can share even less?

B Well, as you like. Maybe I am even a bit of both. A sceptic and also something of a mystic, although rather more of the former than of the latter.

A I must really be grateful for your candour. Many people think like you but are ashamed to admit it. Only through honesty can one get to the bottom of things. And that is what we both really want, is it not?

B Certainly, certainly. I am quite willing to give you my opinion in more detail. But perhaps you had better answer first my objection.

A With pleasure. You see, modern science does not only offer us such high-grade abstract results as the fundamental equations of physics. It also makes available an immense store of empirical facts. The character of all scientific statements lies undoubtedly in their comprehensive character yet the degree of universality can really be very varied. If, for instance, the botanist asserts that this or that plant has a perennating root stock, this statement does, of course, not only refer to one single actual plant, but to all actual plants of a certain species. Yet the distinct species which comprises a limited number of well-defined individuals appears nevertheless clearly in the statement, just as the perennating root stock is, in its turn, a collection of concrete things, which agree in a whole number of characteristics.

On the other hand, the abstract mathematical formulation of basic physical laws does not connect such collections defined by a whole complex of characteristics of certain actual objects, but only single characteristics which may appear in objects dissimilar in any other way. Which kind of statement a branch of science arrives at depends to a large extent on the goal of the respective investigation. Primarily it depends, of course, on the given factual reality. For the scientist may not conjure up into reality connections that suit his book. If we want to proceed from scientific knowledge and use scientific methods to arrive at a philosophy, we will

4

find that knowledge which has been condensed into abstract mathematical formulae is not very profitable for our purpose. We will rather have to draw on such scientific knowledge as refers directly to groups of actual things. I take it that you would agree that what I promised would be achieved if I were to succeed in comprehending according to uniform criteria animate and inanimate nature and finally ourselves and our human society. Above all, if I were to succeed in incorporating into such a system the higher human striving for values.

B You must not take it ill either when I say that I cannot follow you so quickly. It is of course not difficult to incorporate the biological unity "man" into the system of the naturally given. I do not deny it. But I cannot believe for a moment that you will be able to jump from biology to ethics. Human society and its ethics appear to be frequently in evident contrast to biological nature. Anyone, if he were but honest with himself, must admit to having felt this rift in his own breast. It seems that this contrast cannot be eradicated, and it would be difficult to refute a conclusion about its fundamental character.

A I would like to elaborate my thoughts on this matter and I even hope that I can convince you that what you call the jump from the biological concept to the ethical concept is not one of principle but only one of the jumps that occur in nature in other respects as well. I must ask you, though, to be patient, because it will be necessary to go further back.

B I will not be impatient, especially if you will listen to my objections. Before we start, however, I have a question of a much more elementary nature. You have just made a distinction between two kinds of scientific statements. On the one hand, those that relate groups of actual separate things (I think you even spoke of individuals), and on the other hand, those which relate only to characteristics of actual things. You make it quite clear that such relations must always comply with reality. You seem therefore, without reservation, convinced that such objective reality exists in fact, not only in imagination.

A I am indeed convinced — just as I am convinced that we are, in many cases, able to influence the objectively existing world around us by our actions and are able to reshape it within limits according to our ideas — quite apart of the fact that an involuntary influence by ideas, or indeed processes of consciousness, is brought to bear on our surroundings simply because all mental processes are nothing but a functioning of brain cells, that the brain (as part of the body) is in constant reaction with the rest of the body, the body, in its turn, with the surroundings. Thought alone may cause, for instance, an increased pulse rate, a blush, and thus results in a larger emission of heat to the surroundings. I cannot see that our opinions can differ on this matter.

But in every other aspect I consider it pure nonsense that the scientific objekt of research depends on the subjectivity of the investigator, although the latter is, by the way, by no means a new contention. Honestly, I am surprised that you as a physicist have been lured into these pitfalls.

B I would only be too happy to be able to accept your opinion. However, it is not only because I have occupied myself with the various philosophical systems doubting the objective existence of the things surrounding us that I am undecided. No, the reason for my indecision lies just as much in my familiarity with certain recent results of scientific research.

A You have in mind no doubt the "physics of elementary particles", especially the contradictions between the simultaneous corpuscular and wave nature of these particles, have you not?

B Quite. You are, doubtless, familiar with the question this raises.

A Is that, by any chance, the reason for your mystical inclinations? In that case it would be desirable to go a little deeper into these physical problems in order to clear the matter up.

B The root of my mysticism, as you call it, lies in knowledge arising from scientific results as well as in philosophical considerations. We both know that, at one time, the philosophy of enlightenment believed it possible to derive ethics purely from reason. Hardly anybody nowadays is convinced that such an experiment could be successful. I, for one, believe that the roots of ethics go deeper than reason.

A So do I — the question is, however, are these roots of ethics of a natural or a supernatural character?

B We will talk about that later. In the meantime, I admit that a certain inclination to the supernatural has at least been fostered by reasonable doubt of the objectivity of the object of scientific research. The connection is quite simple. It is a fact that we do not exist in a chaos of disorderly sensations, but that, behind all our experiences, be they of the "inner" or the "outer" kind, there is a principle of order, the nature of which humanity has tried to fathom at all times. In former times, one usually assumed a general, supernatural, personal divine creator. Later on, the laws of nature were to provide the sole general principle of order. Personally, I was brought up in the latter conception. It is only logical that, at present, as purely scientific explanations are open to doubt, religious concepts appear acceptable again.

A You consider it proven that scientific and religious concepts and explanations must needs be in opposition on principle, like enemy parties, and the defeat of one is of immediate advantage to the other?

B I do think that history at least shows this antagonism to be permanent, in any case, since free thought has existed at all. I do remember, for instance, that the court which condemned Socrates to death accused him of having taught that sun and moon were not gods but stones. This accusation, by the way, he denied with indignation.

A   I think you start here from a wrong assumption. The antagonism between religion and science did not exist always. Historically it only appears when religion has entered into a decline and has become merely ceremonial. The Greek religion, for instance, had entered into this state for quite some time when it began to see danger in Socrates' scientific way of thinking.

B   You must admit that the gulf between knowledge and faith cannot be bridged because the one is governed by emotion, the other by "ratio", the cold and dispassionate reason. Did not Tertullian say: "Credo, quia absurdum" — or do you not consider the old ecclesiastical teacher competent in this matter?

A   If reason and emotion become opposed, not only in the breast of the individual, but in the public consciousness as well, then there is something wrong with one or the other or both of them.

   Let us look closer at history therefore. In primitive society, you find that priest and scholar are always one and the same person, as it is even to-day among the most primitive tribes where the priest or medicine man carries within himself the entire knowledge of his people, and that was also the case in the most ancient high civilisations that we know. It is typical that under such original conditions the religion is always more or less a nature religion; i.e. the natural forces themselves are really considered to be divine and to be the source of existence, and not supernatural beings existing outside nature. You are probably aware that the conception of gods in human form appears only at a comparatively late stage in the development of religion. Before that come the deities in animal form, and there is an even earlier stage where no such images are formed, but sun, lightning, fire and earth are considered divine, that is, the motivating force of all being.

B   If that were true, it would mean that all original nature religions would indeed be nothing more than the most primitive expression of a purely scientific approach to all things. Now I remember, by the way, having read in a monograph that a similar change of the image of the gods can be traced in Greek coins. In the work, the representation of the Egyptian gods with animal heads but human bodies is considered to be a sign of transition from one state to the other.

   On the other hand, I know that the phase you mentioned, the phase of nature religion, is frequently considered a phase of magic, transcendental interpretation of nature. That is just the opposite of a scientific view of nature.

A   I know the point of view, of course, but I consider it mistaken, at least as far as the beginnings of human civilisation are concerned. The distinction between the material and the transcendental, the natural and the supernatural, is, I am convinced, the invention of a later time, particularly any attempt to explain the material and natural in a transcendental and supernatural way. In earliest times, e.g. times of nature religion, the endeavour was surely not to explain natural occurrences by falling back onto magic and mystery; rather to explain, in a natural way, the many mysterious occurrences that surrounded man everywhere. The fact that mistakes were frequently made, and wrong conclusions drawn, is another matter, quite understandable really.

B What you say appears plausible to me, although I am not sufficiently versed in the history of religion to trust myself to give a final judgement in these matters.

A By the way, the ancients knew quite a few things through their so-called magic or god-symbolic study of nature which, at a later stage of scientific study of nature, were for a long time wrongly considered to be superstitions, a slander for which succeeding scientists had to apologise. I am thinking, for instance, of the fact that Egyptian priests determined the sex of the child in the womb by regular hormone examination without having any conception of hormones. In our enlightened times we had to consider this practice superstitious until we started to explore, ourselves, the secrets of hormones. Sometimes, I cannot help thinking that such a rehabilitation will be extended to other superstitious conceptions.

B You sound quite like a mystic, after all.

A There is no danger. I rely only on what I know — and that is after all much more than the ancients were able to know.

B What is your opinion of the historic development of the Greek and Egyptian images of the gods which I told you I had read about?

A I do not know the pertinent paper, but consider correct what you have quoted from it. I am even of the opinion that the animal and human images of the gods owe their existence everywhere only to a conscious religious policy. We ought surely not to underestimate the power of abstraction of the ancient thinkers and creators of religions. They needed the outward images least for themselves, but to win and frighten the masses. The Graeco-Roman antiquity gives us a further example along these lines, apart from the trial of Socrates, which you mentioned earlier on. Here, you can note the decline of religious conceptions from the level of the primitive scientific system, via the animal and human symbolic one, going on even further and arriving, finally, even at the deification of the political heads of state. For these, temples were built and sacrifices made — quite a frequent practice also in the Orient, by the way. Thus religion proved itself openly to be a pure instrument of power.

B   Which it tends to be to-day as well, among other things.

A   Unfortunately not only among other things.

B   How do you assess, under modern conditions, the deeper relation between religion and science, between faith and knowledge, or rather, what should this relation be like at present, when it would appear that both parts, religion as well as science, are going through a time of crisis?

A   My opinion about this is quite simple. I think that science must and can be our "religion" together with art, about which we will have to talk later. I do not consider that science is going through a serious crisis as you seem to assume. Making science our guiding star, I believe it to be, in reality, no more than a return to the original state in which science in its entirety and religion are one and the same thing. I consider that to be a more natural and more healthy state than the antagonism between knowledge and faith, which has ruled our civilisation for the past two thousand years.

A decisive difference between the original nature religion, and modern science taking the place of religion, lies, it is true, in the fact that the latter does not force us to fill in the gaps in the organised positive knowledge with vague divination, chance discoveries or even plain errors in quite the same measure as our ancestors of the ancient, highly developed civilisations.

B   I note that we have returned to my original question, whether it is fundamentally possible to find a way to the realm of values starting from the natural sciences without taking recourse to metaphysics of some kind.

A   We have, above all, digressed from the intention to occupy ourselves a little more closely with questions of quantum physics which constitute, after all, for you a considerable stumbling-block — or do you consider further discussion about this superfluous?

B   If you are interested in my opinion, which hardly differs from what has already been said in connection with the theme, then I will gladly expound it. I propose, all the same, that we adjourn the continuation of our quite sufficiently extended conversation. We will have to touch on questions concerning the theory of cognition. I would like to brush up my knowledge about this subject to match yours.

A   You do me too much honour. I am no real philosopher either.

9

FIRST PART

Science and Theory of Cognition

Second Dialogue

In this, quite a few separate questions are touched upon, all of which are linked with the main problem of the discussion, viz. whether modern quantum physics leaves any room for the concept of an objectively existing reality. B enumerates the characteristics of elementary particles which, in his opinion, argue against such a reality. He attempts to interpret it along the lines of Kant. He is disturbed by the generally proclaimed invalidity of the causality principle in the "microworld" of the elementary particle and by the lack of "individual identity" of the particles. A believes that, in essential aspects, Kant's theories are in contradiction with the latest findings of physics. He objects to the fact that unusual properties of elementary particles should be considered as a sign that they have no objective existence. In his opinion, one can talk about the invalidity of the causality principle but with regard to the special formulation of that principle that arises out of the physics of continuity. He would like to bring back into favour the older formulation of the causality principle which, in his opinion, finds its belated justification precisely in quantum physics. And its applicability in the physical "micro-world" is beyond doubt. In this connection, the concept of the "islands of reaction" is introduced. B admits that the results of quantum physics do not suffice to substantiate a fundamental doubt in the objective reality of the surrounding world.

A I understand that our discussion to-day is to be about a problem which partly concerns physics and partly the theory of cognition. You had intended to prepare yourself for it.

B I will certainly try to give as short a description as possible of the doubts that disturb me here, so that I can learn the sooner how you intend to deal with the various disturbing properties ascribed to the elementary building blocks of matter and energy by modern physics.

There is, to begin with, the simultaneous wave and corpuscular nature of these particles, i.e. the coupling of two characteristics which have hitherto been considered incompatible. The attempt to reconcile them with each other by interpreting the wave-function as a probability distribution unfortunately leads, however, to the realisation that the causality law cannot be valid in the realm of the elementary particles.

Equally disturbing is the so-called correspondence principle. It is widely confirmed by experience, yet it claims no more and no less than that, in certain cases, the behaviour of the elementary particles conforms simultaneously with two incompatible theories: modern quantum mechanics and the "classical" continuum theory.

It seems, furthermore, that in contrast to the coarser macroscopic structures familiar to our senses, these particles have no stable individuality.

For instance, it has been declared that it is impossible in principle that an electron or a light quantum could be distinguished in any way from another one of the same kind. All this unfortunately gives the impression that all these light quanta, positrons, neutrons, neutrinos and what else they may be called are nothing but the figments of mathematics, devices to help us arrive at the desired mathematical result, but which have no concrete equivalent that exists objectively in reality.

Although I am no philosopher, I know that Kant in his famous work *The Critique of Pure Reason* has developed the penetrating thought that we are unable in principle to see the objects around us as they really are in themselves, but only as we perceive them through our senses and our intellect. He stresses that the form in which things are perceived and recognised is always decisively determined by the subjective conditions of perception and recognition. This statement fits the behaviour of the elementary particles extremely well. Depending upon the experimental conditions chosen at will by the experimentalist, they may appear in wave or corpuscular form, as energy carriers, but timeless, in motion, yet in no fixed position, in a fixed position, but of indetermined velocity. What Kant has claimed so boldly for all objects of nature seems as good as proven by the elementary particles. That is to say, they have no reality as such that does not depend on the experimental conditions chosen purely subjectively.

As, however, all matter perceivable through our senses is ultimately nothing but an aggregation of elementary particles and processes between them, it seems that the objective existence of all nature, studied by us in science, becomes very doubtful — quite in keeping with Kant.

A And yet the same Kant states that causality, although no attribute of objects as such, is nevertheless a necessary condition for the perception of the very nature which does not exist "as such". This, in his opinion, applies equally to the existence of objects in three-dimensional space and one-dimensional time independent of space.

However, the elementary particles, especially in the form in which our present day knowledge presents them, do not fall into Kant's fundamental categories of cognition, nor does their position in respect of the concept of space and time fall into these categories. Their state has to be treated relativistically, at least if they move at great speed, which is certainly not an infrequent occurrence. In that case, as you know, one-dimensional time and three-dimensional space are not independent of each other. So, in fact, the results of modern quantum physics do not really agree very well with Kant's theories.

Honestly, I am surprised that you do not rather seek support in the philosophy of positivism. After all, Ernst Mach did argue at one time that it is a mistake to call it an illusion that there is a break in the pencil which is dipped at an angle into water. According to him the observations only are real exactly as they are made, and the pencil which is straight in air is simply not straight any more if we dip it into water. This theory seems to fit the phenomena of quantum physics like a glove, and dissolves all difficulties in one go. Don't you think so?

B   Now you are pulling my leg. The fatuous story of the pencil being "real" straight or broken is not new to me. I have, however, never liked it. I am very serious about these things and would be only too glad if one could explode this philosophical fantasy. Of course, that would create for science the inevitable task of disposing of the existing difficulties by purely physical means as completely and quickly as possible.

A   You see, now you have really put your finger on the vital point for the evaluation of the attempts at philosophical interpretation of the latest results of physics. All these complicated philosophies, that are so difficult to understand, have just one thing in common: they call a halt to all research in physics by declaring that the apparent discrepancies are discrepancies in principle and cannot be avoided — rather as physics teaches the engineers that the attempt to construct a perpetuum mobile is an insoluble problem and therefore useless. However, it is very doubtful whether such philosophies are qualified to play a similar role of tutelage to physics as physics to technology.

In any case, from all I know, whenever there have appeared such discrepancies they have been an incentive to start new discoveries in physics and I think it is fortunate that the physicists are not being deterred by the philosophical wisdom, but extend their researches into the "forbidden territory" all the same. If they did not we could certainly be sure that the questions open now would remain so for ever, as some philosophising physicists would prefer it.

B   I, too, believe that physics will not be seriously restricted by philosophy; but now I wait impatiently for your counter argument.

A   You have touched on quite a number of widely different points. With which shall we start?

B   I don't think it would be unprofitable to have a more detailed discussion about Kant's theories, or, if you like, about the positivistic theory of matter. However, I am personally most perturbed by the lack of individuality of the elementary particles and their independence of the law of causality, not forgetting the correspondence principle, which is after all a slap in the face for all scientific tradition.

A But why? In my opinion, the correspondence principle is less a statement about the nature of the elementary particle than about the relationship between the two theories which have been formulated to explain the elementary process, i.e. the continuum theory, and the quantum theory which postulates discontinuity. The fact that the correspondence principle has been confirmed by experience in a number of cases means no more than that the quantum and continuum theories remain fundamentally related to each other, in spite of their apparent contradiction. This allows the new theory to draw on the old one occasionally, at least while its own structure has not been entirely completed.

B You think, therefore, that the correspondence principle will become superfluous sooner or later as our knowledge progresses?

A It should be dispensable before long as a logically necessary building brick of the theory, — not so quickly, however, as a heuristic principle leading us to new knowledge and helping us to understand proved results.

B What do you think about the lack of individuality of the elementary particles and the inapplicability of the law of causality for the individual elementary process? Do you believe that this too is only a question of temporary assumptions which are certain to give way to sounder knowledge in due course?

A Yes and no. To begin with, I think it is a mistake to mix, as you do, the concepts of individuality and objective existence. With your permission, let us call the world of ordinary objects directly perceived by the senses the "macroscopic" world. Here, the particular difficulties of the "micro-world" of the elementary particles do not exist. Yet even in the "macro-world" there are phenomena which show us that the two concepts of individuality and objective existence do not necessarily belong together. Let us disregard the objections of certain philosophers and for the time being consider as existing really and objectively such things as, let us say, a certain stone or a tree or a chair. In that case, we cannot deny the same objectivity to an ocean wave or a cloud in the sky. Cloud and wave, nevertheless, cannot be considered to have individuality in the same sense as stone or tree. This possibility is excluded by the fact that the wave, and frequently the cloud too, consists of different particles changing all the time. Apart from that, both show a type of change of shape and form which is foreign to the individual objects mentioned earlier on. Finally, it is incompatible with the characteristic of individuality that two waves that cross or meet add up, as you know, in such a way that they cannot in principle be separated or distinguished from each other at the place of superimposition.

B I can see what you are driving at. In quantum mechanics elementary particles are described by functions which represent standing waves or "wave packets". Therefore, you think, we cannot take exception if we allow them, in spite of their lack of individuality, the same objective existence as the macroscopic waves.

A Quite right.

B I admit that at first this thought appears to be tempting. However, to my mind it does not really go to the bottom of the question. We can only admit the objective existence of the "macroscopic" wave if we allow its material carrier, e.g. water or air, to have objective reality. We know nothing, however, about the carrier of a wave-function, which is described, say, by an electron. The only thing certain at present is that its amplitudes represent probabilities, and that can hardly serve as an argument for the objective character of waves. We can consider probability to be nothing more than an expression of the insufficiency of our subjective knowledge. As soon as we acquire this knowledge, the probability is turned into certainty. In that case, the existence of the wave is entirely subjective. On the other hand, we can divest the probability function of its subjective element and consider the inherent uncertainty and indeterminacy as given objectively and in principle. That makes it even worse because, in that case, we cannot consider the elementary particles to obey the law of causality, which of course seems to call their objective character in question. In any case, we are, after all, accustomed to use the causality principle as the very criterion of reality. Take dreams, for instance. We distinguish between them and reality by the fact that in dreams causality is partly abolished.

A I think you come to these pessimistic conclusions because you make unnecessary assumptions. The probability amplitude has after all been incontestably substantiated by experiments. So why exclude, right from the start, the possibility that the probability amplitude is based on the amplitude of oscillation of some physical quantity as yet unknown? Imagine the elementary particles "smeared out" over the whole space, as the unlovely technical term has it. That the probability of finding, say, an electron in a particular spot is larger or smaller means no more than that the tendency of this elementary particle to engage in an interaction at the point is larger or smaller. The macroscopic standing wave shows the same inclination for interaction.

It is small at the nodal point and large at the crest. Take a violin string, for example, which we can touch at the former but not at the latter without altering the character of the oscillations. It is well known that a certain measure of uncertainty is always attached to macroscopic measurement. It arises from the fact that the measuring instrument reacts upon the quantity to be measured. The measurement, therefore, must be inaccurate in principle, and can only be made more accurate by decreasing the transmitted energy. It is but a natural and ordinary consequence of quantization that one cannot continue to improve the accuracy by reducing the size of the measuring energy *ad infinitum*. Where the whole action to be measured is small, as can happen when elementary particles are involved, this minimal, irreducible action transmitted at the measurement constitutes a considerable uncertainty of the result of the measurement. I really cannot see why similar relations, when they are discovered in elementary particles, should suddenly lead to more profound philosophical conclusions than when met with in the macroscopic world. Don't you agree?

B Your last remark is, of course, basically correct. Yet, doubts about the objective existence of the external world were uttered in philosophical quarters a long time before one knew anything about quantum mechanics and its special problems. I have never claimed that the phenomena of the micro-world *only* lead to the above doubts — rather that these phenomena are well suited to increase existing doubts.

By the way, nothing of all that you have pleaded has dissolved the difficulties connected with the invalidity of the causality law for the individual process. Far from it, your observations seem rather to strengthen the view that they are not confined to the micro-world only, but that, on closer inspection, they are equally to be found in the macro-world, even though the percentage of the occurring uncertainty is much smaller.

Do you, by any chance, mean to escape the conclusions that the causality law is invalid for the individual elementary process by attributing the uncertainty inherent in the probability function to the purely subjective factor of ignorance, that is, ignorance of some hypothetical factor needed for closer definition of the process? That does not alter the question of the objectivity of the individual elementary process.

A Indeed, I mean that there is no need to consider this uncertainty as anything else than a result of our ignorance of the details of the respective elementary processes. For that matter, neither do I think that the objective reality of the individual process becomes doubtful by the introduction of the "subjective factor" as you call it. Nor am I willing to admit that the doubt of the objective reality of the process would be proved correct, if, against all expectations, it is found one day that the said uncertainty is in principle of an objective character.

B Perhaps you would not mind explaining to me first why you hold that the purely subjective limitation of the probability function is no proof, that processes, specifically described up to now only by this function, have no objective reality?

I must tell you what I think is the crux of the matter. As I see it, it is the fact that the scientist is, as you know, at liberty to exact a variety of answers from nature by the manner in which he puts the question, that is, according to the experimental arrangement he chooses in each case. That is to say, he shifts the uncertainty from place to place; indeed he may even stress either the corpuscular or the wave-character of the elementary particles.

However, the result of an investigation of macroscopic phenomena is in any case considered "objectively" assured only if it can be obtained again and again independent of the method of investigation used and it is impossible to obtain contradictory results. To me, it would still appear that the subjective factor is identical to the one Kant has in mind when he speaks of "non-existence-as-such", and of nature being conditioned by our means of perception and cognition.

A I, on the other hand, believe that Kant would turn in his grave could he hear that real and apparent contradictions in results arrived at by different material experimental arrangements should now serve as proof for the validity of subjective limitation of all our knowledge of nature. All arrangements of material experiments form just as much a part of material "nature" as the objects to be investigated. Therefore all results arrived at through these arrangements are no more than the results of reactions between various objects of nature. Kant would certainly have declined to draw conclusions from such reactions about the relation of all objects of nature to the subjective conditions of cognition or to the hypothetic reality existing "as such".

Let us leave Kant in peace for the moment; we will have to come back to him later. It is not correct either, as you suggested, and as one hears it often said, that it depends only on the will of the investigator whether corpuscular or wave nature of the particles predominates or what is the nature of the uncertainty of the elementary process in each case.

Where is the investigator who can force the light to show its wave nature in the rainbow or the electrons running from sun to earth to make apparent the corpuscular nature of the Northern Lights?

Here, as in the laboratory, it is clearly the material conditions of each case that lead according to strict laws to the various results.

It has, of course, nothing to do with the problem that interests us at the moment that the scientist creates laboratory conditions whereas the conditions that produce the rainbow and the Northern Lights are fixed. He can choose the laboratory conditions because he and his assistants have not only a comprehending spirit but also a pair of hands which are capable, subject to certain processes in the brain, of influencing the material external world.

19

Don't you think that in all this there is not the slightest support for assuming the putative dependence of the material external world on the conditions of perception and cognition of our mind?

B I confess I have no ready answer for that, in any case, not until I have had time to consider your reply at leisure. Perhaps we could come back to this point later.

Meanwhile, I would still like to hear why you believe that it does not affect the objective reality of the separate elementary process even if it were to be proved that the character of the uncertainty in quantum mechanics is of a fundamental nature. In other words, why won't you admit the validity of the causality principle as the criterion of reality?

A Frankly, I cannot answer this question until I have made an attempt at analysing the concept of causality.

Nowadays we, as scientists, understand causality to be the unequivocal determinacy of each separate process of nature. In the classic, continuum physics it is the result of fixing the starting and marginal conditions of the solutions for the differential equations in question; that is, in physical terms, the result of the influences, which the closeness of the nearer environment exerts on the process concerned.

We must be aware, however, that there exists another version of the causality principle. It may be more primitive, but it is in certain respects more meaningful. Popularly expressed, it means roughly that "everything has its cause". It is not at all equivalent to the concept of causality meaning determinacy. A consequence of the latter concept, especially in the form developed in continuum physics, is that each event is brought into causal relation with every other event in the world, provided that it does not lie outside the time-space cone determined by the light velocity where, in any case, distances in space and time only serve to diminish the degree of interaction.

The second version of the causality principle contains a statement which is in some way a contradiction of the first version. It nevertheless corresponds without doubt to the facts. It is the statement that the accomplishment of most (in popular usage even all) events is not affected, or a least only imperceptibly, by every other event. It is only affected by certain events, which are called the "causes" of the event. It means this: to predict an event, possibly not quantitatively but certainly qualitatively, it is generally sufficient to know a few discrete and at the same time typical interactions of physical theory from amongst the infinite number that are interwoven to form a continuum. The fact that we can usually manage in our daily life without constant precise measurements and calculations clearly shows that this principle is quite generally valid and is sufficiently reliable in practice.

B I don't quite see what you are getting at. Do you intend to use the existence of certain discrete cause and effect relations instead of the principle of the universal causal determinacy as the criterion of reality?

A I just wanted to make sure that when you talked of causality as a criterion that allows the distinction between dream and reality you did not by any chance have in mind the scientific principle of the quantitative causal determinacy. Dream experiences are even less an object of quantitative determination than events in actual daily life. You must clearly have thought of the characteristic of many dreams, that certain discrete cause and effect relations, known to us in conscious life, appear not to obtain.

B Does that not boil down to the same thing? The macro-world yields the law of causality in either form as a result of the natural laws assumed to be valid in it. The qualitative version propagated by you clearly applies even less in the micro-world of the elementary particles than the usual scientific form. I can therefore really not see what is the advantage for the solution of the question we are interested in at the moment in bringing up this conception, correct in itself, as I will readily agree.

A You ask what is the advantage of such a conception?

Well, to begin with, I hold that it can be applied in the micro-world. That should refute your argument in which you maintain that the objective existence of the elementary particles is doubtful if it cannot be applied. We have seen that in the macro-world, at least, we are accustomed to use the "popular" version of the causality law as a criterion for reality, rather than the scientific principle of complete determinacy.

What is much more to the point, however, is that it is precisely quantum mechanics which enable us to begin to understand the existence of cause and effect relations in the macro-world quite independent of the fact as to whether they exist in the micro-world or not. One cannot, after all, deny the immense importance in practice of these relations for our everyday life, our technology and our science. No more can it be denied that the cause and effect relations form a foreign body in continuum physics not in absolute conflict with its laws, but not satisfactorily explained by them either. I also think that the sole reason why the principle of discrete actions is practically ignored in the scientific world-image up to now is that the cause and effect relations form a foreign body and are inexplicable in principle.

B That is clearly worth a further discussion.

A I propose we take it step by step. Perhaps you will be kind enough first to explain to me why you consider the principle of discrete relations not applicable in the micro-world.

B I think that this is a very simple point. Let me give a few examples to avoid the danger which lies in abstractions. Let us say I pick up one of two stones and work on it with a hammer. I will presumably be able to break it up. In that case the hammer blows are the cause that breaks it, you agree?

A Certainly, that is just the sort of thing I had in mind when I talked about the existence of discrete cause and effect relations.

B In the same way, some time after the snow has melted in the Alps, the Rhine and the Danube for instance will rise at Bonn and Regensburg, the water-levels will rise as an effect of the melting of snow in the mountains earlier on. On the other hand, the Thames and the Congo do not rise correspondingly nor does the stone that has not been hit by the hammer break. Stone and hammer, water and the different rivers are all individual objects and I think I am right in assuming that precisely their individuality and their consequent stability are necessary conditions for the creation of the discrete cause and effect relations, which have been observed between them. That being the case, there can clearly be no question that elementary particles which have no individuality of this kind can be carriers of analogous cause and effect relations. Symptomatic of dreams is that not only do we find that cause and effect relations do not obtain, but also that cases of individuality are cancelled. For instance, a particular person seems to change into another in front of our eyes. That seems to indicate to me that causality and individuality are inseparable.

A I don't agree. True, discrete interaction-lanes cannot be formed without the stability of the affected macroscopic objects. This stability causes, so to say, the majority of the arriving action currents to bounce off the said objects. But I would not say that this requires individuality based upon a dissimilarity of objects of the same kind by which they can be recognised and not mistaken for each other.

That, however, is exactly what the micro-world demonstrates to us, as it contains very stable formations which nevertheless have no individuality. They effect and suffer actions exactly like macroscopic "objects". We have only to think of the Wilson chamber, where we can follow the path of a single elementary particle by its condensation trail. In exactly the same way we can follow the route of a plane by the vapour-trail, although the plane flies so high that it is more often than not invisible itself. Is not that almost a textbook example for discrete cause and effect relations? It does not matter that the uncertainty of the impulse of such an elementary particle is directly proportional to the definition of its path, since it is a characteristic of the "popular" causal principle that, for its application, no complete or approximately complete knowledge is needed about the data of causes leading to certain consequences. It makes no statement at all about the possibility and accuracy of quantitative measurements.

B   I am willing to accept the argument in respect of the Wilson chamber, that you quoted, and I even admit that it might apply to other cases that you have not mentioned. I recall, for instance, that when we observe radioactive, luminous paint under the microscope, we can actually see the reactions between individual elementary processes. But what about cases where there can be no question of a definite trail, not even of a fixed position of the particle? Then your approach can obviously not apply.

A   Not at all. Since it is necessary only to know isolated, fundamentally incomplete data, which however adequately define cause and effect in each case, in order to enable us to apply the principle of discrete reactions, why not substitute, in cases where a path is missing, the now definable impulse for it in the constitution of a discrete cause and effect relation? I think that an analogous step is always possible. However, even if we do not agree to that, there remains one other circumstance on which I have touched earlier on. The ultimate reason that macroscopic structures are subject to the causality principle of discrete reactions is their stability, i.e. their insensibility with regard to a great many external influences. This stability is clearly a consequence of the stability of the elementary particles, and the stable quantised reaction they enter into with each other. How else could we explain, for instance, the stability, whether mechanical, chemical or electrical, of the crystalline or amorphous molecular structures which are the basis of all solids and fluids? It requires the stability of the molecules and is a result of it, just as the stability of the molecules is a result of the stability of the atoms which is generally the result of the stability of the atomic nucleus. Agreed? In that case I would like to add another remark.

B   Do go on.

A   I would like to point out the special conditions which arise in compound stable structures of the micro- as well as the macro-world. Take, for instance, the atomic nucleus. It consists certainly of simpler components, between which enormous forces are active. The resulting potential wall largely prevents the intrusion of influences from the outside, and conversely the emergence of influences from inside the nucleus to the outside.

B   Excuse me, but I can't understand why you mention this in connection with the principle of discrete reactions! I take it you were thinking of radioactive phenomena when you were talking of the emergence of influences from the atomic nucleus. However, these are only subject to the laws of chance according to our present-day knowledge.

A   Chance is the very thing I wish to refer to. For the time being, however, I hope you won't object if I go no further than to state that action from the inside of the nucleus to the outside and vice versa occur comparatively rarely, at least under the conditions reigning on earth. On the other hand, we can hardly help assuming constant reactions between the various components of the nucleus. This gives the nucleus the character of a kind of closed system of reactions. I am going to call it "islands of reactions". Let us leave the question of determinacy alone for the moment.

B   Qualified like that, I will no longer object to your observations.

A   We find similar islands of reactions in the macroscopic world, albeit not so clearly demarcated. Every material structure and every one of its material components to which the discrete cause and effect relations apply has clearly the character such as an "island of reactions", otherwise no component structure could be stable. This also applies to the compound stable units lying between the atomic nucleus and the macroscopic object. We have mentioned them before: the atom and the molecule. I want to point out that the smaller the compound structure is, the more pronounced becomes its character of "island of reactions".

B   There is this difference, however: In the macro-world the comparatively rare reactions between "islands of reactions" do not depend on chance either, but must be considered to be determined causally in the classical sense in common with all other macroscopic events.

A   True, true. Nevertheless, one is justified in speaking of chance also in the macroscopic world without coming in any way into conflict with the principle of general determinacy. In everyday life, and in the macro-world in general, we talk of chance only when reactions take place between two or more "islands of reactions", which cannot be predicted from the previous history of any of the "islands of reactions" involved, nor from the normal course of cause and effect outside and inside them. We call it chance, for instance, if a roof tile falls just in front of my feet while I am on my customary way to my place of employment. We say in that case: "It could just as well have fallen on my head."

B   I must say so far I have not looked for scientific value in this popular expression.

A   All the same it is there. The tile itself, the roof, and my person, too, certainly represent "islands of reactions" in exactly the sense that we have in mind. The events on the roof are not altogether independent of the weather, but my working hours are. The processes in my brain governing my steps are connected with my working hours, but only slightly with the weather, and certainly not at all with the events on the roof, particularly with whether the tiles were well or badly laid. No more do the events on the roof depend on my thoughts and actions, as I am no tiler. Therefore, notwithstanding the determinacy of all macroscopic objects, it could not be predicted that the tile was going to drop right in front of my feet.

B Simply because, in mathematical terms, the correlation coefficient between the events on the roof and in your body is zero.

A Exactly. However, if determinacy and chance are not in conflict in the macroscopic world, why should they be so in the microscopic world?

B Don't you think that special conditions exist here? As you know, a radio-active atom, for instance, has a probability of decaying within a certain space of time, let's say within the next hour. This probability remains the same, although the atom may not have decayed even after a hundred years. However, if certain inner causes were to exist which determine the date of decay, but of which we have no knowledge, in that case the decay, when it occurs, would depend on the previous history of the events inside the atom. Thus the degree of probability of decay would depend on the age of the atom in the same way as the probability of death depends on the age of the person.

A I think that your conclusion is wrong. It is true that the human body contains parts which have themselves the character of an island of reactions, for instance the atoms and molecules of which the body is composed. However, these are present in such large numbers that even the infrequent reactions between these islands occur generally with a statistical regularity, practically indistinguishable from strict law.

In face of that, we have only to assume that the decay of the radio-active atom is caused by an interaction between only a few, maybe just two, components with properties of an "island of reactions", to be able to think of determinacy and the law of chance as combined within the atomic nucleus as well.

In such a case, the macroscopic equivalent of a radio-active atomic nucleus would not be the human being but, say, a system consisting of machine gun and target. The system flies into the air as soon as a shot of required accuracy hits the centre of the target. The probability of the bull's-eye does, of course, not depend on the frequency with which the machine gun has been fired, apart from the effect this has on the wear and tear of the gun. The probability remains the same at any moment.

B If that were correct one could, by the way, also assume that the greater rôle that chance has in the micro-world is simply a consequence of the sharper definition of "island" properties of the compound micropart.

A Perhaps. However, I would rather assume that here as well some physical circumstances play a part about which we know nothing as yet. But I want to ask you something else now: Don't you object to my having spoken of the human body as an "island of reactions" in the same way as of inanimate objects?

B As long as this observation is confined to the scientific biological aspect of the human body, I don't object.

A I expected this qualification. And what would you say if I were to propose that the so-called "free will" of man can be traced back to a hypothetical existence of islands of reactions in the central nervous system in such limited numbers, that in this unique instance no statistical determinacy can be achieved?

B I think this thought in a somewhat different form has already been uttered somewhere else. Various people have assumed that free will exists owing to the fact, that each act of will is released in the brain by a single elementary process, indeterminate in principle. This hypothesis really seems to have quite a lot to recommend itself.

A I am not so sure that the islands of reactions creating the freedom of will have to be elementary particles. They could easily be islands of interactions composed of many elementary particles similar to those of our macroscopic world. All the same, I am happy to find that you clearly have no misgivings in explaining in this particular case a moral phenomenon — for that is what free will means after all — by a physical phenomenon. After all, you insisted that morals had to be exempted from this type of explanation.

B You are mistaken. Even in this special case I am not ready to equate ethical problems with the biological problem explained by physics. If you consider the elementary process to be indeterminate in principle, and you do not exclude this possibility, then free will can be traced back to a phenomenon which lies outside the general determinacy of natural law.

A I understand. You mean to say that the supernatural quality which you consider necessary for an explanation of ethical subjects is disclosed in the individual elementary process by its very indeterminacy. In other words, you see in it something like the "work of God"!

B I don't really know, ... maybe ... !

A I emphatically do not admit that supernatural, or if you like extra-natural, phenomena are the only means of explaining the possibly fundamental indeterminacy of the individual elementary process, even if I cannot entirely reject the existence of the latter.

Besides, it is quite compatible with the assumption of a general determinacy to assume that the origin of free will lies in the existence of islands of reactions, microscopic as well as macroscopic, in the central nervous system, as I imagine them.

But please let me ask you just one more question before we finish with our discussion for to-day: have I been able to convince you that the recent results of quantum mechanics do not furnish the least support for all the philosophical opinions which doubt the objective reality of the object of physical research independent of our subjectivity?

B I think I can admit that without reservation. Nevertheless I do not think that the question about the objective reality of nature "outside us" has been answered conclusively. After all, quantum mechanics does not disprove the considerations which have led to the doubts about this reality long before the particular laws of the micro-world were known. I think it will be worth while talking about general questions of the theory of cognition next time.

A I agree.

Third Dialogue

*A attacks the so-called "critical" direction of philosophy. He accuses it of
leading in the end to a contradiction with practice. He shows that even the
so-called "moderate" or "scientific" positivism does not show a way out of
this difficulty. In his opinion, philosophy should not proceed from the least
possible number of assumptions, but from as many assumptions as the
various sciences are capable of supplying. Philosophy should also make use
of scientific methods.*

*B does not wish to pursue the path of criticism beyond Kant's philosophy.
He rejects the positivism of Mach as well as the philosophical systems of Fichte
and Hegel, yet whe wishes to retain the starting point of positivism. He be-
lieves, nevertheless, in the possibility of cognitions not depending upon ex-
perience. Yet, on the whole, he keeps a more or less open mind about the
arguments of his partner.*

B   As a result of our last conversation I have once more perused the first
    part of the *Critique of Pure Reason* and have tried to become clear
    about the essence of the fundamental thought it contains. It is really very
    simple. All our concepts of reality are subjectively conditioned. They
    cannot represent the objects as they are without reference to the observer,
    because we cannot receive an impression of the external world except
    through our senses. We are altogether unable to recognise anything that
    does not correspond to the special conditions of recognition which are
    necessarily given by our ability to recognise. I find that this general
    thought had not been shaken by any of our considerations so far. Indeed
    it is hardly refutable.

A   And I declare that it is simply a vicious circle. Why on earth should the
    subjective recognition not be suited to the objective reality best of all?
    We have all the more reason to assume this if we consider that all activi-
    ties of perception and recognition are a function of the brain. Why should
    this be the only organ that is not equal to its given task? Why should it
    be less equal to its task than, let us say, our stomach to its appointed task
    of digestion? A satisfactory function of the ability of recognition can
    obviously exist, after all, only in the fact that it provides us with correct
    concepts of the world around us, existing "as such" objectively and inde-
    pendent of our function of perception. For this, nothing else is necessary
    than that our senses and the mechanism of thought connected with them

are adapted to the objective matter approaching them from outside in the same way that our gastric juices are adapted for the arrival of food. To assume the opposite, like Kant, means assuming what is to be inquired into.

B I do not consider yours a valid argument. The brain is, after all, exactly like the stomach and our whole body, an object of nature, a part of the experienced world which is according to Kant already adulterated because it is experienced by the subject. It is, therefore, in principle, not permitted to operate with these factors to disprove Kant's postulate, because one would have to assume from the start what was to be shown, namely that Kant is wrong. You yourself have upheld the opinion that reactions between objects of the experienced world may, in principle, not be used as support for Kant's postulate. If that is so, then they cannot be cited either to prove the opposite.

A You are quite right. I had no intention of proving the contrary. I only wanted to draw your attention to the invalidity of Kant's conclusion. I am furthermore surprised that you do not pursue your criticism even further. Kant's ideas do not presume organs of sense, yet he presumes senses, not brain yet the ability of recognition.

Are these assumptions not very daring? Is it not even more daring and even very inconsistent of Kant to speak about the object "as such", of the object of which, on his own evidence, he knows nothing? How can he dare to assume even its bare existence?

B That far I would not like to go — that would be going too far.

A But one must go so far if one adopts the critical mode of thinking, from which Kant has started out. The positivistic philosophers who followed did go that far.

B That would mean the collapse of everything.

A Not at all. Of course according to this way of thinking, nothing remains as certain reality except that which is given as the immediate content of consciousness. That is little, but after all something. Of the external world it is not much more than the knowledge of an infant of a few days.

B What is your intention — do you want to defend or deride positivism?

A I simply do not want to be hazy about the consequences to which it leads. Are you, for instance, familiar with the meaning of the word "introjection" used in positivism?

B If you think it ought to be in the interest of our discussion, explain it to me, please.

A Kant accepts, unquestioningly, the elementary differentiation between object and subject. The positivistic philosophers, however, pursue their point of view quite consistently and arrive at the conviction that even this differentiation is an adaptation of the material of sensation and perception. The latter alone is immediate and undoubtedly given. They call it "introjection" if one attributes to sensation and perception a sensitive and perceiving subject as carrier. The character of the subject is, therefore, as derived as that of the perceived object.

This conclusion can certainly not be avoided if one wants to continue with Kant's way of thinking without succumbing to solipsism, or some such concepts which are really quite mystical and unscientific — for instance, the concept of an impersonal, purely spiritual subject, or the also purely spiritual but "objective" idea.

B   Nevertheless, I think I would believe that it is not necessary to go to such extremes. Solipsism, the theory that only the personal "I" exists in reality, but that other I's are already fictitious, is surely generally considered to be a curiosity. You probably meant Fichte and Hegel when you spoke of philosophers pursuing the way shown by Kant's philosophy. Their teaching may have caused tempers to run high in their time, but in the meantime they have lost much of their persuasive powers. The same seems to be the case with the extreme version of positivism as taught by its founders in their time. If one takes it seriously, then any scientific research, and specifically any research in physics, yes, more than that, any activity, will become absolutely impossible.

A   E. Mach felt something similar himself. He admitted at one time that we, acting beings, can neither dispense with the I-concept, nor the concept of the bodily reality of the objects around us. In another place he expresses the opinion that particularly the physicist must put aside certain results of positivism in the course of his research and let himself be guided by opposite views, views which positivists condemn.

B   Don't you think that a philosophy is not worth its name if one must forget it in order to practise physics or pursue any practical activity whatever in this world?

A   That is what I think. But what about quantum mechanics? At one time you were of the opinion that one must begin, in the newest branches of physics, with quite different assumptions from those of classical physics, particularly with respect to the question of independence of the object of research of the investigating subject.

B   I have never shared Mach's extreme views as far as I was familiar with them. Apart from that, you have taught me in the meantime that quantum physics does indeed not take up an exceptional position in the question of the objective reality of our object of research. There is, however, another rather more modest version of positivism. This version does not lead to unacceptable conclusions, or conclusions which cannot any more be taken seriously, although it is not able to give an answer to important questions. There is a trend in physics which is called positivism, too. It demans that any explanation of immediate experimental results and measurement results are quite consciously dispensed with, and it considers only the immediate results as ensured recognition. True, I have so far considered this way of thinking somewhat unsatisfactory. It does, however, undoubtedly display a healthy critical tendency.

A I, on the other hand, believe that a philosophy that may not be pursued to the extreme is worthless as well. What, after all, is "directly" given as a result of measurements and what is "interpretation"? We both know, after all, how measurements are taken in modern physics. The occasion when, for example, the effects arising from elementary particles are observed directly as in the Wilson chamber, or in the fluorescent microscope, are really the exceptions. What, in fact, is mainly observed, also in the realm of macro-physics, is the deflection of some galvanometer or manometer. The actual measurement result is arrived at by sundry calculations inspired by considerations which would not be possible without a certain interpretation of the direct observations. It appears that one cannot arrive at any result without a certain measure of interpretation. Therefore I consider the "moderate" or "scientific" positivism an impossible philosophy. I am, furthermore, of the opinion that it is a mistake to attempt to trace back everything to elementary sensations, this being the only thing undoubtedly given according to consistent positivism.

B I think the fundamental assumptions of the positivistic philosophy are less unsatisfactory than the difficulties which one obviously has in proceeding from such beginnings. It is, after all, the nature of philosophy that it approaches things with as few assumptions as possible. It is simply forced to search for some starting point which is undoubtedly given. I am not so sure that to take sensations and perceptions as the last elementary components of all our conceptions of reality is actually such a bad starting point. I do admit, though, that the previously mentioned moderate positivism suffers from the fact that the "measurement results" and the "direct experimental results" that are to be its support have generally lost their elementary character of perception, let alone sensation. Thus, it becomes difficult to establish in each case where the undoubtedly given stops, and interpretation begins. However, these difficulties are no proof that the starting point of the positivistic way of thought is wrong.

A In my opinion, it is not only that the choice of starting point for positivism has been unfortunate — perhaps more about that later — but that it is a mistake in principle for philosophy to start, as you have so rightly said, with as few assumptions as possible. Or put it this way, philosophy must restrict itself to assuming the minimum of "what is undoubtedly established" and "which is directly given". To this everything else must be traced back if it is to find a place in the system of such a philosophy.

B I, on the other hand, cannot imagine at present how philosophy as funda-
mental knowledge can start otherwise.

A To avoid barrenness, or getting bogged down in endless difficulties,
philosophy will just have to employ the scientific method of research. It
is, on the contrary, the nature of this method to assume as much as
possible by imagining as complete a picture of the research object as
possible, by employing all available data and searching for verifiable
conclusions about the conceptions which are, for the time being, to be
considered merely a working hypothesis. According to the measure in
which these conclusions can be confirmed and are proved to be correct,
the hypothesis may be counted a true theory of reality. If necessary, it
will have to be altered so as to have a claim to accuracy. When interpret-
ing new phenomena, one will, of course, always try to manage with tested
theories to begin with.

In this way one avoids arriving at a theory which has to be put aside for
specialised research. Quite the reverse, the results of "specialised" sciences
will become part of the firm basis and building bricks for such a philo-
sophy.

Thus I believe, for instance, that it is quite meaningless to occupy oneself
with the theory of cognition divorced from psychology and the theory of
the origin of the species.

B That means that, in your opinion, philosophy is not there to furnish a
foundation for the specialised sciences, but that, on the contrary, philo-
sophy can only be founded on the specialised sciences.

A Indeed, I am convinced of it.

B I really ought to be in favour of such a programme for philosophy, being
a specialised scientist myself. All the same, you know my fundamental
doubts about the possibility of arriving in this way at a complete structure
of philosophy, particularly with respect to the system of values with
which a philosophy has to occupy itself.

A I have indeed promised to give you an answer to that, but at the same
time, I also asked you to be patient.

B My patience has not been tried yet. However, quite apart from this fun-
damental doubt, I cannot even get accustomed to the idea of an inductive
philosophy, neither can I free myself so quickly from the concept that it
is the essence of philosophy to progress mainly deductively.

A I expect you are thinking of the method used in geometry and mathema-
tics in general — "more geometrico", as Descartes has called it.

B You must admit that the Descartian method has subsequently influenced
more or less all philosophies; even those which are in their inspiration
diametrically opposed to Descartes' way of thinking. That proves, after
all, that it is endowed with quite a special power of persuasion.

A I believe this to be the very method which has led to making conclusions in a vicious circle. Even the "cogito ergo sum", "je pense, donc je suis" is the first example of such a fallacy. This is not formally apparent in the Latin version, simply because Latin does not require the personal pronoun, "I think" — "Je pense": The existence of the "I", the "I am" is already presupposed in this sentence and if it reappears once more as the final conclusion in the formula "I think, therefore I am" we have before us the classical form of a vicious circle.

Pure logic does not lead to anything that has not been assumed in some form or other; and if one wants to come to many conclusions one must make many assumptions.

B Nevertheless, the deductive method has actually led to many brilliant results in mathematics.

A That is only because the fundamental concepts of mathematics have, without doubt, been taken from experience — a large, varied experience.

B I think this statement requires more thorough substantiation. Up to now, I have not been of that opinion. I will not deny that, in some important cases, the mathematical, fundamental concepts have been taken, so to say, from nature. — I am thinking, for instance, of the Leibniz-Newtonian calculus. However, if we take, for instance, Riemann's "curved spaces", we see that, vice versa, a concept entirely divorced from experience, born purely of the mind, has been used later to comprehend natural phenomena which were far from anyone's mind in Riemann's times. It really seems that we have here the case of the human mind dictating quite literally the laws to nature.

A Before anything else I want to state that the scientific method which I risk recommending to philosophy is not altogether a purely inductive one. In physics, for instance, the new conclusions of a theory which have to be proved eventually by experiment must be arrived at by deduction. This deductive part is no less important than the inductive one. I was only against the idea that a purely deductive method could be used with success in philosophy. The origin of all deductions must necessarily lie in some fundamental concept and axiom or other that cannot be defined or derived any further. Such fundamental concepts and axioms must stem from experience if they are to have any sense. Only as far as they are taken from experience will the conclusions drawn from them coincide with experience.

Mathematics itself demonstrates this very clearly to us. The most elementary fundamental concepts in mathematics are certainly the number and continuum. From what, then, does the concept of number stem? Undoubtedly from the experience that nature works generally along the principle of duplication and produces everywhere discrete, stable and comparable units, e.g. individual objects, which we can perceive with our ordinary senses. These almost force the concept of number on the human mind. Do you not think that our ten fingers are the root of the decimal system?

B Maybe! Yet history has recorded various other systems of number of which we find traces even to-day, for instance, in the calculation of time and in the English system of weights and measures.

A I do not deny it. The main thing is, however, that the concept of number itself can only be drawn from physical reality, e.g. from the existence of similar but discrete objects, particularly solid bodies.

B You may be right if you look at things from the historical point of view.

A As its name conveys, geometry stems undoubtedly from the surveying of land, just as the continuum on which geometry is founded stems from the physical experience about structures consisting of a great many elementary particles by which we are surrounded in everyday life, you agree?

B What is your attitude, however, to Riemann's prophecy of a future physical experience formulating geometrical concepts which did not correspond with reality as it was then known?

A Riemann's concepts rest, after all, on the same fundamental concepts as the rest of mathematics. That later on they proved to be useful for the description of newly discovered natural processes means nothing else but that these processes are, in essence, not as different from earlier known facts as is sometimes claimed.

B In tracing mathematical, fundamental concepts back to experience, you apply, so to say, an historical mode of observation. Do you not have to admit, though, that these concepts could claim a right to an intellectual existence quite independent of experience, and that, in principle, they could also have been discovered independently of experience, purely according to the laws of the mind?

A I cannot admit that at all. The laws of our mind represent only the rules which have to be considered regarding intellectual work if our brain is to fulfil its biological function. This function is nothing else but to register correctly — i.e. according to reality — the external world existing independently of the mind and consequently to distribute the appropriate impulses to the rest of the body. In the same way, the biological function of our legs is the locomotion of our body, and that of the intestines is the digestion of the food of which we have partaken. Thus far, our mental processes are not at all autonomous, but are obviously decided from the beginning by the structure of the external world that is to be registered, and by the character of the experience that is to be made.

Neither are there any other rules in mathematics, and therefore there is, to my mind, no sense in the concept of "a right to intellectual existence independent of any experience" — whether in mathematics or philosophy.

Furthermore, the lack of definition of the fundamental concepts forces us to stick to reality with respect to them in the case of any deduction in which the fundamental concepts are involved in one way or another; otherwise changes in their content, i.e. serious errors of thought, might occur. We did agree, did we not, that there is no other possibility of establishing the fundamental concepts?

B In the case of philosophy you obviously think that it must collect its fundamental concepts from various specialised sciences.

A True, true. That is, it has been the task of philosophy to generalise these concepts and the statements connected with them, to achieve thus a connection between the so-called humanities and science.

B You do pose a very extensive and grandiose task to philosophy. It is, so to say, to play the part of a supreme science, ruling all other sciences.

A That is not quite the right definition. Its subject-matter should not be other sciences, but the subject-matters of all sciences in their entirety.

B I understand. That is by no means a lesser goal.

A It means of course a constant task, a task that never ends.

Fourth Dialogue

A confesses to be a supporter of the materialistic image-theory of cognition. His aim is to find fresh proof for it in the results of psychological experiments, and in our knowledge about the origin of the species.

He believes that an extended version of the biogenetical law of Haeckel is also valid for the development of the human perceptive faculty, and he derives from it a method of investigation to be used in the theory of cognition. He analyses two meanings in the word "spirit" and proves it to be impossible for omniscient spirit to exist. He rejects the concept of supremacy of "mind" or "spirit" over "matter" in any form whatever, as well as the concept of a metaphysical "will" as originator of the laws of nature.

B has nothing against the theory according to which each process of recognition means construction of a material image or model of the object of recognition in the brain of the recognising person. A defeats B's objection that materialism, which carries the conviction of unique supremacy of the laws of nature in the world, defeats its own purpose and leads to pantheism or to Schopenhauer's metaphysics of will.

B   To return from the general to the specific: you remarked, in our last discussion, on the particularly close relations between the theory of cognition and psychology, and the theory of the origin of the species. Your arguments have convinced me of your point where psychology is concerned. What, however, has the theory of the origin of the species got to do with the theory of cognition?

   Do you, by any chance, intend to connect the history of the evolution of mankind with the fact that the laws of cognition are dependent on future experience, that is on the predetermined structure of the environment?

A   I think that the dependence can only be understood in the light of the history of evolution. We have some idea of the effect that the environment has on various parts of the body by encouraging or discouraging the use of them in the course of many generations. The brain will hardly develop in a way different from other parts of the body. Developing gradually, it had to adapt its structure and functions more and more to the given structure of the environment, just as the senses connected with the brain have adapted themselves to the given conditions of the environment.

B   I expect you are thinking of the fact that our eyes have the greatest sensitivity at a wavelength which happens to coincide with the energy maximum of the solar radiation.

A Yes, among other things.

B The theory of cognition, however, is not concerned with the historical evolution of the perceptive faculty, but with the conditions for the recognition of the existing world as revealed by the given perceptive faculty; i.e. it is clearly concerned with problems of the moment.

A However, these very problems of the moment are connected very closely with the history of evolution. To understand the former we must refer to the latter. This close connection becomes obvious when you consider that our conscious perception is only one of the many types of learning; that our perceptive faculty is merely a particular — and particularly well developed — form of the ability to learn, which is one of the fundamental qualities of life.

B I don't know that your last claim is justified. The only qualities that I have so far considered to be fundamental are metabolism and the ability to reproduce. Surely, there is no learning without brain?

A I don't think so. Any organism, whether endowed with brain and central nervous system or not, can, after all, react, within limits, to altered conditions of environment by an increased development of existing faculties, and by acquiring new ones. Such a reaction is simply what we call "learning" in the broadest sense of the word. Yet even taken in the narrowest sense of the word it has been proved that "learning" is not necessarily connected with brain by the succesful attempt to train decerebrated frogs and even amoebae.

B Of course! I had not thought of these really remarkable experiments in which regular Pavlovian "conditioned reflexes" were developed.

A Seen in the light of the history of evolution it is clear that the conditioned reflexes of Pavlov are definitely a rather original quality of life. The conditioned reflexes are therefore the very thing with which we must start, if we want to learn what cognition really means. Of course the most important thing for us is not the actual reflex, but rather the coupling of two or more sensorial stimuli for which the observed reflex becomes the outward sign because of the fact that after the coupling has taken place, one stimulus can, so to say, substitute for the other to produce the reflex. For the purpose of "training", the research-worker deliberately chooses the timing of the stimuli, which leads to their association in the receiving apparatus of the reflex carrier. In nature, however, it is the presence of stable objects, and the discrete lines of influence which originate in them, that result in such couplings. In this sense, every coupling of sensations which has been acquired in a natural way represents a model of part of the environment, albeit a one-sided one. In particular, by means of multiple couplings of a larger number of sensations, images of certain objects are formed which are not quite so one-sided any more if such objects have repeatedly affected the various senses of the organism — and so we have before us the first step of actual perception which is to be attained in the consciousness of humans and surely also in the consciousness of the more highly developed animals. We call it "perception" in contrast to mere "sensation".

B That is, you mean to trace back perception in general to the same fundamental phenomenon as Pavlov's conditioned reflexes.

A Existing perception and conditional reflexes can, on the whole, hardly be separated from each other. In any case, such conditioned reflexes in highly developed animals will arise comparatively rarely from a simple coupling of only two sensations, but more frequently from a complicated complex of many different stimuli, which are the very image of particular objects of the external world. I am convinced too that, in the adult, sensation tends to give way to perception entirely. Practically every arriving stimulus of the senses is absorbed into the existing complex of stimuli corresponding to the appropriate real facts. In this way, it is not the stimulus as such which reaches the consciousness, but straight away the appropriate objective property of the "perceived" object which does not necessarily have to coincide always with the received stimulus. Thus, provided we have not been specially trained in a school of painting, we see the leaves of trees always green and a white flower always white, even if colour-photography teaches us that in either case the impressions of colour that reach our retina vary considerably according to the time of day. In the same way one finds that two similar light impressions, if they occur in quick succession in two adjacent places, are "perceived" as "movement", even if no movement has taken place. This is the foundation for the pretty optical illusion whereby a luminous arrow apparently travels trough an impenetrable body. In reality, however, two views of the arrow have been illuminated successively, one just in front of and one just behind the "pierced" body. In this context, it should also be considered that the simultaneous sensation in muscle and sight caused by a movement of the head is always correctly combined for the "perception" of the true state of rest or motion of the objects around us. Under normal, natural conditions of life this automatic translation of almost every sensation into a component of an objective "perception" is of course most appropriate. Possibly only pain and such other bodily sensations that are not caused by external circumstances can avoid this translation — and even in this case concrete conceptions obtrude forcibly, e.g. when we speak of "burning" pain.

B Earlier on, you talked about the progressive retreat of sensation in favour of perception in the adult. Do you think that this relation is different in child and adult?

A In my opinion Haeckel's biogenetic basic law is also valid for the development of the perceptive ability. This states, as you remember, that each individual goes roughly through all the stages of evolution in the course of its development. Man in particular is still in a very primitive stage when he first sees the light of day. The human baby contrary to exsessorial birds and animals, whose young soon follow the mother, has certainly no perception in the first hours and days after birth, only sensations and unconditioned reflexes attached to some sensations. Accordingly he has not yet any idea of the real identity of the tactile, optical, and acoustic sphere of stimuli. One can even follow in detail how he achieves the perception of the objects around him and the conception of the three-dimensional space together with the first insight into certain primitive cause and effect relations. This is surely analogous to the way in which our pre-human ancestors achieved such insight in slow evolution. Organised abstract thinking is of course only developed much later in connection with the acquisition of a fund of concepts — language. The original image — or model — character of cognition on which perception is primarily founded is, however, always preserved in principle.

B Surely you know that what you have just said is identical with the fundamental concept of the so-called materialistic theory of cognition?!

A Certainly I am aware of it, and you will also have the opportunity to observe that it is not only my opinions regarding the theory of cognition that are materialistic. By the way, the image theory of perception, admittedly in a very primitive form, is ancient and in no way solely accepted by materialistic thinkers, but by Aristotle and Plato as well.

B We are quite well informed about the function of the sense organs. Where, however, the theory of perception is concerned I don't expect you mean the word "image" or "model" to be taken literally, and it can hardly be your opinion either that the model of a three-dimensional object is repeated in miniature in our brain, etc.

A Of course, I don't picture the formation of a model in such a primitive manner. Considering the higher forms of cognition which go beyond simple impulses, we find that these models are not only built up out of sense-impulses and objective qualities that correspond to sense-impulses, but undoubtedly also out of more or less abstract qualities which are, strictly speaking, defined by analogous connections between concrete objects. Such models cannot possibly have the crude character of a small scale three-dimensional model of the object, if only for the reason that the modelled object itself has often no spatial extension anymore.

B I am in principle also an adherent of the modeltheory of cognition. However will brain-research ever achieve a direct proof of the existence and kind of such a model? This subject is, after all, unimaginably subtle.

A Why not? I can think of no statement more irresponsible than the apodic-
   tic "ignorabimus". However great the progress of research may be, we will
   certainly always stay in the position of having before us an unlimited
   field of the unknown — but to maintain that any particular point in this
   field must remain unknown for ever is not justified.

B To return to perception once more. You are convinced that, in the case of
   exsessorial birds and young animals that are immediately able to walk,
   the coupling of sensations which is the foundation of perception takes
   place before hatching or birth respectively, that is, at a time when the
   coupled sensations cannot even have been present?

A Why ever should that not be the case? The ability to move their extremi-
   ties in a coordinated manner so soon after hatching or birth shows that
   the couplings which allow them to do so must have been made in the
   brain at a time they could not be realised by the embryo because of its
   restricted position. In the human infant on the other hand, the various
   intellectual abilities lacking in the beginning are, as you know, only
   developed by training. This holds also for the perception and the first
   general insight into the physical structure of the world around us that is
   connected with the perception. At first the infant's own fingers are instru-
   mental in this, and after that above all the well-known rattle, which helps
   the child to combine the sensations of sound, touch, sight and muscle in
   a coupling-complex, which makes a correct model of the objective thing
   with respect to its three-dimensional appearance and certain primitive
   causal relations to other objects. So you see, the rattle represents a very
   valuable aid to the acquisition of the first knowledge about the objective
   world. The childish intellect does indeed proceed quite logically in this
   game. It is even my opinion, that for the philosophical theory of cognition
   also there is no other beginning than simply this: one must be clear about
   this kind of origin of certain fundamental concepts and repeat the process
   of acquiring them consciously. It is difficult not to accuse a philosophy
   of a certain infantilism if it stops at such primitive knowledge or, worse
   still, at only part of it, and refuses all further experience gained by im-
   proved means to be able to endow the primitive knowledge with absolute
   value.

B This unflattering remark I suppose is meant for positivism when it de-
   clares sensation or perception to be absolute, or for Kant because of his
   aprioristic conception of space and causality.

A The apriorism of Kant's concept of time is no better substantiated either.

B You mean, the child also acquires it only gradually?

A I would not say that. Perhaps man has an inborn concept of time as
   chickens, calves and foals have an inborn sense of three-dimensional
   space with its absolute axis of preference indicating "above" and "below".

However, in this context that is of no importance. We had, I think, realised that all categories of thinking must originate from experience. If inborn, their origin lies in the experience of the ancestors. My remarks, however, were not only aimed at positivism and Kant, but also at the so-called "critical" philosophy as a whole which must of necessity arrive at an infantile origin as they go backwards in principle when searching for the fundamental of cognition. The critical philosophy makes, however, one further mistake in choosing the subjective factor as its point of origin — for instance, the subject itself as does Kant, or the facts of sensation as do the positivists and Hume. The logical process of cognition, as every child demonstrates to us, leads to the subjective, i.e. to self-knowledge, only after the cognition of the objects around it — and even later to the cognition of individual processes in its mind. It is very characteristic that self-knowledge of every child begins not with the use of the little word I, but by referring to himself by first or pet name. The child simply learns to understand and label himself as an object like other objects, that is to say from the "outside", long after he has grasped the objective reality of the mother and other persons. And long after the complete annexation of the "I" concept comes the statement about the processes in his own mind, always still exclusively in the impersonal form. For a long time the child never says: "I am happy" or "I am sad" or "I am hungry" but refers to the origin and aim of its emotions: "The object is beautiful" — "The toy has broken" — "Give me to eat".

Actually it is impossible to understand the personal I in any other way than by comparison of one's own person with other persons, and a statement about one's own mind comes last. The great difficulty is that the comparison with another person is not really possible. For once the dependence in principle of the observed object on the observing subject — claimed by some philosophers for all cognition — really exists and makes it extremely difficult to acquire a correct judgement.

B I don't know whether positivism in particular really deserves the reproach that it starts from the subjective. Like the child, it puts sensation before the concept of the subject. You called that logical a moment ago.

I must admit that again I cannot see how positivism, starting from such a quite acceptable beginning, comes to the dead-end which we discussed earlier on. I am thinking of the incompatibility with practical life and research which becomes obvious when one pursues its reasonings consistently.

A Were positivism to start from the content of sensation as the child does, then the road to further cognition would be clear. But positivism does not do that. It considers the sensation-process to be the alpha and omega, and this really cannot but be and remain a purely subjective phenomenon

41

even if the concept of "I" as carrier of this phenomenon is not explicitly assumed.

B I would like to return again to the fundamentally materialistic character of your conclusions about the theory of cognition. It is the basic conviction of materialism, which I'm sure you share, that it is *only* matter that is a primarily given property. By comparison "mind" in any form can only be considered as a derivative. This is in complete accord with your strict rejection of the subjective as the starting point for the theory of cognition. However, what about the laws of nature? Is materialism not self-contradictory if it ascribes to them an objective absolute character independent of the investigator? The contents in particular of the most general natural laws is after all of an absolute, abstract — mental kind. Neverthless, they govern matter, as their very name implies. To accept them in materialistic terms means really nothing else than that the primacy of the subjective "spirit" over matter is substituted by that of an objective "spirit" over matter. I really cannot see how the acceptance of such a primacy differs from the faith in an omniscient ruler of all things, provided he is considered to be impersonal, in the way of pantheism.

A I think this question is solved quite easily if we make it clear what we mean and are allowed to mean by "spirit" and "matter". To begin with, the word "spirit" is used in two quite different meanings. Having so far spoken repeatedly of the "perceiving subject", we have thereby already dealt with one of the two meanings of the word, and we both agree, I think, that "spirit" in this sense can only exist as the function of organised matter, preferably of a brain. It is therefore always dependent on matter and not the other way round. A perceiving "spirit" divorced from any living organism, particularly an omniscient "spirit" of this kind, whether personal or impersonal, is obviously a nonsensical idea, just as impossible as the supposition that a proper digestion can take place without stomach or an equivalent chemical system.

Even more unthinkable is, of course, an omniscient "spirit" appropriately bound to matter. The "material" model of the world, which would have to be the foundation of such an omniscient "spirit", would have to mirror *all* properties of the known world, and consequently would have to be identical with a second edition of the entire world. This conclusion would render the entire concept absurd. At all events, it is impossible to construct primacy of a perceiving subject in this way.

The second meaning of the word "spirit" is simply a combination of certain qualities, essential in some way or other, of a real phenomenon, preferably, but not necessarily, created by men or of man himself or of a group of men. It is characteristic of the concept "spirit" in this sense that it never contains within itself all the given properties of the observed object, but only a selection excluding all those that are of no importance for whatever combination is being considered at the time. A subjective element is introduced into the second meaning of the word "spirit" by the fact that this combination is more or less arbitrary.

It can, of course, not be denied that the laws of nature, as we formulate them, have essential qualities of this concept of "spirit", particularly as there is generally more than one way of selecting the properties which are contained in a particular formulation of a law of nature. However, the very criterion of a correct formulation is that the conclusions about matter which are drawn from it must agree with those drawn from other equally correct formulations. The behaviour of matter does not, therefore, depend on the subjective element in the various formulations that are occasionally possible and so one cannot in this respect, talk about a primacy of the subjective perceiving "spirit" over matter either.

Let me deal with the concept that matter is "governed" by laws of nature as such independent of any perceiving "spirit" as assumed by materialism. This concept also is not tenable in this form, nor can it lead to the assumption of a primacy of an "objective" spirit over matter. Only a matter which is formless and chaotic in itself could be "governed" by laws of nature or be subject to them. Such a concept of matter, however, is not supported by experience and is altogether without physical content. A hundred years ago it would perhaps still have been possible to see such "formless" matter in the "substance" endowed only with inertia and weight. To-day we know, however, that the material world consists of particles some of which are endowed with mass and others are not. Yet both kinds of particles show in their simultaneous corpuscular and wave-nature a very complicated form of organisation without which they would be inconceivable. Can you suggest another physical meaning for the concept of a chaotic, formless mass, independent of the reality of the elementary particles, which justifies the differentiation between a "governed" and a "governing" principle of nature?

B Your argument then comes to this, that matter, free from the law of nature, does not in fact exist and is not conceivable. Yet the conception of the polar contrast between a "governing" law of the spiritual kind and matter which is "governed" by it does not assume at all the separate existence of either member of the polar pair, neither in reality, nor in imagination. It is obviously a philosophical abstraction, a distinction in thought only, which could be reasonable even if it were not observable and could not be translated into practice.

A The only reason for such a concept would be that it helps to make us understand a phenomenon which could not be understood in the same way without it. Yet where is such a phenomenon? I don't know of one.

B I cannot name any particular phenomenon like that, but couldn't it be that such a concept would help us to understand the sum of all .phenomena, i.e. the world as a whole?

A I think that nothing more is at the back of the dualism of such a concept than an anthropomorphism for which modern science leaves no room. When man uses the axe on a tree trunk or sends the trunk through a frame-saw to transform it into planks, the tree trunk, to be sure, appears to him with respect to the intended purpose as unformed raw material, and the plank as the result of the effect of his organised will which has imposed its law upon the raw material. This approach, however, has meaning only with respect to man. It is, and remains, pointless for nature on the whole and without regard to human affairs, which should in any case not be part of the concept of an "objective" spirit as you see it.

I think that the expression "laws of nature" is not altogether a happy one. By analogy we associate law and law-giver, i.e. the will that formulates the law. However, we cannot assume such a will without lapsing once more into anthropomorphism.

B That depends, surely, on what you understand by "will"?

A You don't expect me to give you a definition of will, do you? It is a phenomenon given by experience. It is, however, like the perceptive faculty, always connected to a living organism.

B Wouldn't it be possible to give the concept of will a broader sense, so that it would be suitable for the originator of the laws of nature, divorced of all personality, of course?

A That brings you into Schopenhauer's metaphysics.

B I don't express these thoughts in the form of a statement but in the form of a question. Should the answer be positive, I would not be afraid to agree with Schopenhauer. Nor would I reject the materialistic concept ·if I thought it correct.

A You don't really believe that a satisfactory solution of fundamental philosophical questions could be found by an eclectic method, do you? On the contrary, we had, had we not, come to the ·conviction that one ought to be able to demand of any philosophy that it may be carried through consistently ·and without having to draw on others.

B I think so. Our discussion hinges after all on the question as to whether it is possible to work materialism out to the end consistently, without getting entangled in contradictions. However, what is your attitude regarding my question? Is there, or is there not, in your opinion, the possibility of a reasonable expansion of the concept of will in the way I have mentioned?

A I quite believe that human will represents nothing but a specific form of general facts of nature which may even contain inorganic entities. Though, to call this general concept will, is certainly wrong. As wrong as calling the form of communal life of the ants an ant-colony, which is certainly not a colony — but more about this later.

By the way, don't you think that the topic we have taken for our discussion to-day has been sufficiently explored and that we can postpone further arguments?

B   You have indeed succeeded to-day in answering some of the questions which have puzzled me for a long time in such a way that I at least cannot refute them. Yet I am still not satisfied where the complete presentation of your own scientific-philosophic ideology is concerned. Anything you have said on this subject has only transpired occasionally when talking about quite different subjects. Furthermore, we have not progressed one step in the fulfilment of your promise, to explain the world of values without metaphysical aid.

A   You did, did you not, mention right in the beginning the old trinity of the true, the good and the beautiful? It was your opinion that modern science had made at least the first of these values questionable because according to widespread opinion they excluded the concept of objective truth, independent of the subject. And don't you have to agree that no tenable argument in favour of this pessimistic opinion has remained after our discussion?

B   I have already admitted that I cannot support any more my original opinion. However, perhaps our discussion has by now progressed so far that we can occupy ourselves with the question of good — that is, the domain of ethical problems. We have not even touched on these things.

A   If you agree that we have dealt sufficiently with the questions of the theory of cognition for the moment, we might devote ourselves to the ethical problem before anything else at our next meeting.

SECOND PART

The Ethical Problem — Nature and Culture

Fifth Dialogue

In this dialogue the discussion turns to ethical questions and B, to begin with sets the tenor. He thinks that the idea of good as a tenet for practical actions is religious in character, and is, as is all civilisation in his eyes, in irreconcilable conflict with the rational explanation of biological nature and its demands. He sees the roots of human morals in an irrational, and at the same time an absolute and inner, "urge for the good" which is supposed to be independent of any outside conditions. However, it does not appear without contradictions within itself, and is incapable of exhaustive definition. For several reasons he strongly opposes Kant's ethics.

A rejects Kant as well, and shares B's opinion that ethics in the end are always founded upon man's struggle towards values. He does not, however, recognise a supernatural, metaphysical source of this struggle. He opposes the argument that ethical demands are absolute, and points out the historical fact that human morals change. He sees no difference between the impossibility of an exhaustive definition of the idea of good as well as all other cultural ideas of man, and the well-known impossibility of a complete definition of any living body. He equally contests the opinion, uttered by B, that all culture is basically incompatible with biological demands and has, as an unavoidable consequence, a decrease in biological viability.

A To be able to approach the question of values, in particular ethical values, in a scientific manner, we must first of all agree to treat the inner phenomenon "value" as purely conditional on the laws of nature. Should we not succeed in arriving in this way at a satisfactory understanding of the problems connected with it, then the scientific approach would have to lay down its arms.

B You had stated at the outset, remember, that you did not intend to fall back on metaphysical concepts in your observations. I still think, though, that where ethical values are concerned, merely understanding the object to be investigated is not enough, and that no ethical investigation can be considered satisfactory if it does not produce a feasible rule for practical action as well as theoretical insight.

A I agree absolutely.

B And this is where my fundamental doubt begins. I would say that, basically, no investigation whatever that is based purely upon reason, including the scientific method, can arrive at an ethical evaluation of concrete, selective actions except when a suitable, general ethical principle is available and has simply to be applied. This investigation cannot, however, establish such general principles in the last analysis. It seems to me that things here compare with the proof of all other general philosophical statements. However, as you have said yourself, in the sphere of the merely descriptive sciences, we always have to rely on experience, but in the realm of ethics we obviously have to rely on the existence of a moral demand. As a principle this cannot be proven by reason. If you do not want to deny the existence of such a demand, you must allow for it and therefore introduce an irrational element into your scientific philosophy after all.

A You and I concur in the opinion that ethical investigations as well must rely finally on a starting point which cannot be proven by logic. You, however, are convinced that this irrational element, as you call it, has a metaphysical character at the same time, and is therefore not open to a scientific approach. Why should this irrational element not equally belong to experience?

B I do not know, but I would say that all experience can in principle give information only about that which is, not that which ought to be.

A I cannot agree to that. A value only becomes a value when it appears to us to be worth striving for. Do you agree that a striving for values that belongs to the inner experience really does exist? If you do, what would your objection be if I declared that this very striving is the empiric starting point of all ethics? Could it not be that an essential part of this investigation is the very attempt to fathom the character of this striving, and above all to explain its connection with the entire nature, inside and outside, of man?

B I think that we are now coming to the vital point of the whole question. I am, of course, not of the same opinion as Kant, which even Schiller ridiculed, that action engendered by every directly experienced drive must necessarily be ethically inferior. On the contrary, I believe that the striving for good indeed exists as an original impulse of the human heart. What I cannot believe is that this striving, obviously aimed at something of a sublime nature, can be satisfactorily explained by the natural sciences, and that it can be brought into line with all the other human impulses — for example, with those that correspond to the instincts of animals.

A In other words, you see the "striving towards good" as something particular, something sublime, standing outside the rest of the natural order?

B In any case, I perceive human morals to be foreign to nature, and that ethics and the dependent problems are particular to man alone in the living world.

A Surely you do not assume that anything which distinguishes man from the rest of the living world must needs be considered different in principle from the rest of nature? Do you think, for instance, that organised human language is a phenomenon that cannot be explained as a normal biological development? To avoid misunderstandings, I feel it is vital that at this point you should try to state very clearly the reasons which influence you.

B   I must point out that I doubt the ability to explain the ethic phenomena biologically simply by intuition. I also have, however, various arguments based on reason, and if you think it important I will try to explain them. You say, for instance, that language is a purely human achievement. That is indeed correct. Nevertheless, we find even in the animal world the beginnings of language development, and many domestic animals can regularly even be trained to understand human language in a passive way, although of course they cannot speak actively.

On the other hand, it seems to me that the appearance of an ethical element is a step of a much more fundamental kind. All those human impulses which can be explained biologically in one way or another, or even compared directly with the drives of animals, are doubtless always of the limited kind. They are not equally strong in all human beings, nor are they quite similarly orientated. They depend on age and sex, and their actual occurrence depends on the circumstances of place and time which excite them. They do not even remain the same for one and the same person during his lifetime. On the other hand, the concept of "good", if it is to have any sense, must be considered as an absolute principle, always consistent within itself and not dependent on place and time or all subjective factors.

A   You know yourself that your last argument is quite in line with that of Kant whom you have criticised so recently. He also attempted to define "good" as an absolute principle.

B   You mean the famous formula of Kant's "categorical imperative" — "Act always so that the principle of your actions may always serve as general law?" No, I did not have that in mind. Kant's statement seems to me to lack one important thing which is that it can only be applied to actions that conform to principles. Yet I think in the real human society that consists not only of philosophers there occur very many actions. "good" in the ethical sense, which do not follow principles, but arise in fact directly from an original impulse which drives towards "good". I am very much inclined to consider those actions irrational since they evade any exhaustive definition. On this point I do not agree with Kant who repeatedly stresses that, in his opinion, reason is the only source of moral action. I rather follow the ancient faith of humanity which has always connected morals with religion.

A   You are thinking of such ethical principles as, for example, the Christian brotherly love which is also described as "higher than any reason".

B   I have several objections to the moral teaching of historical religions, and in particular to the "love" ethic of Christianity. Perhaps we will talk about them later. Neither do I like the fact that present religions will always rely on revelations which are supposed to have happened in historically distant times under circumstances which cannot be investigated, and which are usually anything but credible. However, the true "revelation" of a higher principle may not be so remote and is simply identical with the inner voice crying for "good".

A   What do you say to the change that morals and morality have undergone in different times and different civilisations, all of which can be proved historically? I think it shows us that the "inner voice" can turn out to be very different according to different external circumstances.

B   I expected this objection, but it is not a sound one. You confuse the absolute principle of "good" with its forms of moral and morality, and these all too often and in many places would be better called immoral and immorality. The manner in which they change is a subject for the history of civilisation. I think that the same history of civilisation shows again and again that a protest against the historical forms of morality is particularly felt when the gulf has become too great between them and that which, independent of times and circumstances, the human heart feels to be "good" and "right".

A   And how do you imagine that the gulf between the two opens, that is between morality and what you say is "good" and "right" independent of time and circumstances?

B   That is a subject for history pure and simple. I am sure one would find that the reasons for the decline of morality have nothing to do any more with morals in the higher sense.

A   I must say I am of a very different opinion. At the same time I believe we will have plenty of opportunity to talk the point over and I suggest that you continue with your line of thought, which I have interrupted with my objection.

B   There is another essential point which, in my opinion, argues the religious foundation of ethics. The ethical questions are, after all, not only inner ones, but at the same time outer, social questions which cannot be solved practically without a certain social restraint. I see no possibility in justifying such restraint without assuming a higher, ruling order free from all subjective and other limitations.

A   If I understand you correctly, you do not really want to found ethics on religion, but the other way round, religion on ethics. Let me retrace your argument. The scientific-biological explanation and substantiation of the demands of ethics is not possible, therefore only the religious foundation remains. The religious foundation is required because of the necessity for an explanation of ethics which are common and compulsory.

That was initially the mainspring of the mystical inclinations frankly admitted by you at the beginning of our discussions, wasn't it, leaving aside your opinions, now discarded I take it, that modern physics leads to the supernatural?

B   We have talked in detail about science and religion. However, as regards the ethical roots of my "mysticism", as you call it, you have not yet extirpated them and you have just expressed my argument for them rather well.

A   Again, like Kant, you are trying to prove religious concepts by ethics. As you know, having found all proofs of God impossible he finally "postulated" God's existence as well as the immortality of the soul, so that good deeds should find their reward in another life since, as shown by experience, they are all too often only poorly rewarded on earth.

B   I, however, cannot see the least connection between this idea and my reflections. I have the feeling that there is something second rate about it and it sounds particularly odd in Kant's mouth; he who usually declares so emphatically that any action loses its moral value if it is motivated by any personal advantage whatsoever. Is not the strong desire for reward after death in fact a question of an advantage of a highly personal nature? If not, why then is the quite personally intended immortality of the soul prerequisite to the receiving of reward? I think that the religious postulates of Kant show only one thing clearly — that the thought of actual, final renunciation of reward for the good deed appeared unbearable to him after all, and that reward is an indispensable incentive.

A   On this point we agree entirely. I also find that Kant's ethic is ambiguous and as inconsistent as his theory of cognition. However, since you do not agree with Kant, what are the religious conclusions you draw from the ethical premise? Or would you rather not say?

B   Why not? As a child I believed in a personal God and a life after death, because in those days I had been taught to do so.

I lost this faith even before my formal scientific eduacation. However, in the definition of the "higher principle", I must admit that I cannot go further than to say that I assume that the "moral must" which man feels in his breast is its ethical manifestation.

Therefore I am all the more interested to hear from you, how you propose to arrive at the understanding of ethical values and how you are going to formulate practical rules of moral conduct without the assumption of such a "higher" principle.

A   You said earlier on that you have several reasons for doubting the biologically, natural character of moral striving. Perhaps you would not mind finishing your arguments before I specify my own conceptions.

B I want to say, above all, that, in my opinion, man is, independent of any philosophical reflection, directly and naively conscious that his ethical motives are something very particular and different from anything else. Impulses or drives which can be explained biologically are shared by man with the animals. Ultimately their aim is the same. It is self-preservation and preservation of the species. Altogether, they form an harmonic whole, more or less well balanced, in which fundamental conflicts cannot occur. Yet, it is one of the most elementary, moral experiences that the ethical challenge does not fit very well into this whole, and is often enough even in sharp conflict with it.

A I expect you are thinking of the dilemma between the impulse of self-preservation and military duty in war, or the restraint, which custom, at all times and of all people, imposes upon the exercise of the sexual impulse.

B Exactly! However, I think the difference between ethical and biological impulses goes much further than your examples imply. Even you will have to admit that a deep and unbridgeable gulf exists between our whole civilisation and biological nature and its demands. As human morals are clearly part, and an essential part even, of this civilisation they must necessarily be, as a whole, in deep fundamental conflict with the merely biological, and not only in single exposed instances.

A There I must disappoint you. I agree with you that human civilisation is, in many of its individual manifestations, in conflict with the biological demand. I am on the other hand, in no way prepared to admit that there is a "deep, unbridgeable" gulf between the whole of human civilisation and biological nature. But please tell me what makes you think like that.

B All right — I will be more precise. From the biological point of view what we call civilisation is in many, maybe even essential points nothing but degeneration. It is really based on the diminished viability of the species "man" and its consequence is a further decrease of this viability. If I were to deny seriously any higher point of view than the scientific, biological one, it would force me to consider as a logical consequence that this very culture and civilisation with its ethics, art and science is degenerate. To be consistent I would have to wish for its and my speedy destruction. And to tell you the truth, I think that is going too far, although I know that quite a number of the educated of this world flirt with this apocalyptic thought.

A I cannot agree with you. In my opinion it is not at all true that civilisation in general has to lead to a decrease in viability of the species "man". Consequently the conclusions you draw from this assumption collapse as far as I am concerned. I consider that the concept of viability must in principle be applied only with respect to the environment in which it moves. Fishes, for instance, cannot live on dry land, nor birds under water. In the same way the viability of civilised man can, in my opinion only be considered with respect to his normal environment, that is to say the civilised environment he has himself created and in which his viability is undoubtedly considerably greater than that of many other living beings in their environment.

B   Don't you think that even within humanity the viability of people at a lower level of civilisation is greater than that of people at a higher level — I mean the general resistance in respect of physical stress?

A   I cannot admit that either. It is possible that the Mexican and the Eskimo can endure better heat and sunshine, or cold and temporary starvation respectively, than the average middle European. However, I am sure training plays a big part in such matters and I would not be surprised if the civilised Northerner could compete with the Eskimo and the Southern European with the Mexican in enduring the respective hardships mentioned. Even if that should not be the case, it is undeniable that primitive people generally have a much lower resistance than civilised man to certain illnesses frequent in our cultural environment as, for instance, influenza or tuberculosis. It is at least an open question as to how the respective powers of resistance on the whole would compare. Finally, the higher intelligence is also a weapon in the struggle for existence. This weapon, which means a considerable increase in the entire viability, is incomparably better developed in man, be he more or less civilesed, than in any other living being.

B   As tusk and trunk are much better developed in the elephant than teeth and nose in all other animals, including man.

A   Certainly!

B   I think that we are digressing. I have still other or deeper reasons for my belief that the springs of civilisation are moved by higher powers of a spiritual kind. I think that the spiritual powers simply cannot be biological ones nor be understood on the basis of natural laws, because, as you have stressed in the beginning, the natural laws are completely rational and free of contradictions, whereas there is no rational explanation for the higher ideas which make human civilisation superior to the rest of animate nature, let alone inanimate nature.

A   And in these higher ideas you include the idea of "good" of which you said previously that you are convinced of its irrational character?

B   Yes, indeed. That is exactly why I consider that the conflict between the demands of ethics on the one hand and the biological impulses of the inner man on the other hand is not accidental and confined to single cases, but general and necessarily of principle.

A What do you really mean when you say that ideals cannot be rationally explained in the last resort? I expect you mean to say that you do not think it possible that the essence of civilisation in all its manifestations can be explained to the smallest detail by an analysis of abstract reasoning.

B At least, since the essence of civilisation is irrational, it follows that rational analysis must be impossible.

A However, that is no reason why the general principles of civilisation should not be of an absolutely rational character. You and I have accepted the natural laws to be rational. And yet they do not enable us, as the knowledge of the general laws of nature should in principle, to describe to the last detail for instance one single biological object of nature, nor to calculate it quantitatively in all its functions. However, that does not compel you to conclude that the biological "secret of life" must necessarily be of an irrational character which can in no way be scientifically explained.

B It is not only the question of being able to explain completely in the sense of a rational analysis. It is, as I have hinted, just as much the question of existence of inner conflicts, which in the case of ethics not only appear between the ethical element on the one hand and the biological on the other, but even within ethics themselves.

A In what way?

B Well, I think of the ethical conflict as the case where the demands of ethics, necessarily thought to be absolute and homogeneous, are, so to say, split into two demands of equal weight which are in practice mutually exclusive so that there is no other way for the afflicted individual but to act contrary to one of the demands.

A You think that such inner conflicts cannot occur in the realm where pure laws of nature rule supreme.

B I pointed out a little while ago that the whole of nature outside man certainly does not know anything that can compare with a set of ethical problems. I cannot imagine that inner tensions and conflicts of the same fundamental kind as in ethics can ever occur where natural laws and the ensuing biological singleness of purpose of organisms represents the only ruling order of events. Nature, apart from man, remains virtually at one with itself and in harmony, at least everywhere where it has not been exposed to human interference.

A Before I answer that, I would like to know whether you have now completely explained your point of view.

B Yes, I think so. That is essentially all that I have to say for the moment.

Sixth Dialogue

The discussion returns for a time to a scientific level. A expands on the type of inner harmony which discloses itself in the appearance of very many animate and inanimate objects of nature. He expands the definition of the concept of the physical tension in such a way that it can be applied to living beings. He shows that no material natural structure which is stable and seems to be harmonical, and in particular no living being can exist without inner tension and without the constant occurrence of partial destruction inside it.

B points out the ability of living beings to be activated by influences of the environment in the manner of technical regulators for the purpose of producing and maintaining a fixed ideal state. According to B, this ideal state is fixed for every individual by the common characteristics of the species to which it belongs. He thinks that the degree to which the reproduction of the characteristics of the species is perfected in the individual determines the degree of harmony of its appearance. He proposes to call the sum of these characteristics the "concept of the species". He considers this concept of the species to be determined purely scientifically and not, like Plato, metaphysically.

A is prepared to accept this manner of classification and believes that it permits the definition of the ethical concept of "good" as a part of the "concept of the species homo sapiens".

Understandably this is not an opinion with which B can agree without reservation.

The dialogue ends with an agreement about the way which future discussion must take in order to prove systematically the reliability of the proposed interpretation of the ethical ideals.

A   I expect it is now my turn to make a comprehensive survey of my thoughts regarding the problems which interest us at the moment. To begin with, I would like to pick up the threads of our conversation in which you commented on the pervading harmony of virgin nature. My opinion differs. It seems to me that virgin nature in particular is full of inner tensions and violent conflicts. Simply take a good look, for instance, at any kind of landscape inhabited by living creatures. Is it not in a state of war of all against everyone?

B   Are you thinking of the struggle for light and water between plants and the feeding habits of the carnivorous animals?

A Not only that. You could also have mentioned herbivorous creatures. They sustain their own life only by constantly destroying other living matter, and many other things besides.

B I do not deny that. All the same, apart from the struggle that takes place between individuals, the landscape as a whole breathes the most glorious peace, do you not agree? Is it not this harmony, this lack of conflict in the whole which constitutes the essence of the famous beauty of nature? Is it not that which makes the sojourn in unadulterated nature the best recreation for us poor civilised humans who are tortured by so many conflicts? After all, the war of all against everyone takes place only in a relatively narrow sphere in which the various living beings are in contact with each other. Nor is this contact necessarily hostile. However, if we consider each separate individual we see that any of them, except man, constitutes a special world of high harmony. Yet I really do not know in what sense one could speak of tensions, conflicts and contrasts when one considers the inorganic world, which forms, after all, a much greater part than the whole of organic life together. In it, everything happens harmoniously according to laws which can be expressed in mathematical formulae.

A The laws that rule there can certainly be translated into mathematical formulae. Yet do not the same laws apply to those biological processes for which, as you have yourself admitted, struggle and conflict is characteristic? It seems to me not only that laws of nature which can be expressed in mathematical formulae do not hinder the appearance of tensions and destructions but they demand it. And I think that this state of affairs can be detected by us particularly easily in inorganic nature where the processes in question are much simpler than in the organic world.

B I wonder whether we are not in danger of falling into poetical comparisons and word-play. Of course, I have no intention of denying the existence of mechanical and electrical tensions in inorganic nature, neither do I deny that the material is destroyed when an insulator breaks down or a tension-probe is ruptured. In the first place these processes of destruction hardly play a greater part in inorganic nature than cases of destruction of one living being by another. In the second place, it seems to me that they have nothing to do with the kind of tensions and conflicts with which it had been our intention to occupy ourselves, except if you were to succeed in showing me strictly the direct connection between an ethical conflict and, let us say, an electric tension. At the moment I doubt if you can do that.

A Well, these two things cannot be quite so unrelated as all that. Does not every spiritual struggle take place in the brain? Its working is always accompanied by action-currents and therefore by electrical tensions.

Naturally, I do not imagine that I can convince you by such general pointers. As we want to avoid the danger of falling into poetic comparisons and of shifting the meaning of concepts we must take the trouble of analysing a little more accurately a few concepts which are essential to us. I would like to start with the general concept of tension. To begin with, I would like to bring it into relation with the stable structures of inorganic nature, macroscopic as well as microscopic. As we have agreed earlier, it is the theory of elementary particles which has enabled us to understand their formation to some extent.

With reference to such stable structures — macroscopic objects included, for instance — I think we can agree to understand by tension in general the state in which the structure finds itself because of some specific, causally comprehensible influence from outside, the influence not being so strong as to prevent the structure from regaining its former tensionless state as soon as the influence has ceased. We will accordingly understand by "inner tension" the inner state of a stable composite structure created by the mutual influence of the structure's equally stable components on each other. Would you object to that?

B I cannot say that I can see what you are aiming at but I do not have any objections. Please continue all the same.

A First I would like to establish that our physical definition of tension may also be applied unaltered to the living world. There is no doubt that, for instance, a living individual is a stable structure in exactly the sense we have in mind. That is to say it is a composite structure which contains many components also stable in themselves. Furthermore, any sufficiently big tension leads to the destruction of the structure under tension in the organic as well as in the inorganic world. This fact is recognised by the structure not returning to its previous state after the tension has ceased. The state of tension in a living being can in particular, of course, be caused by the influence of another living being.

B I certainly do not object to considering the living being as a stable structure capable of being put into reversible states of tension by outside influences. However, a closer look at such states will show a quite decisive difference from the inorganic world. Let us see, for instance, how the change in external temperature influences the warm-blooded animal. Extremes may lead to the irreversible damage of parts of the body or even to the death of the whole organism. A more moderate change — for instance, a lowering of the skin temperature — causes some not too great deviations from the normal state. After the temperature influence has stopped, these deviations disappear. As I have said, I have nothing against defining the state of the body caused by temperature influence or the analogous state of the body being infected by a virus as a state of tension.

However, the influences mentioned are to quite a considerable degree not passively suffered influences, but in this case it is a question of an active, purpose-directed reaction which I fail to see even in the most stable structures of inorganic nature.

A You touch on a point about which I had intended to speak. But before we continue to talk about it, I want to make a general remark which applies to the inorganic as well as to the organic world. I would like to establish that it seems that the appearance of tensions in our sense is not at all in conflict with that which you have earlier described as the "general harmony" of nature.

B Not so long as destruction does not occur, or at least does not go beyond a certain point.

A That is where we differ. I declare that the tensions and destructions with which we actually meet in nature do not disturb the overall harmony of stable structures or structures composed of stable parts. Why, they are even a constituent part of this harmony. The latter could neither be created nor last without them.

The overall impression of harmony which, for example, the natural landscape makes on us is, I would say, essentially dependent simply on the repetition of groups of similar organic and inorganic components within it and also on a certain regularity of arrangement. That this materialises at all and lasts for any length of time is certainly a consequence of the close interlacing of the normally discrete action-currents which connect the components of the whole with each other, and on the similarity of influences which consequently affect similar components. These may mean, in individual cases, either reversible or irreversible tensions.

B I agree with that in so far as reversible tensions are concerned. The irreversible alterations, however, mean destruction every time and can, I feel, hardly add to the harmony of the whole. They surely cannot produce a peaceful, harmonious impression of the whole if they are prevalent.

A I don't agree. First of all, I think you are making a mistake in equating peacefulness with harmony in nature. Are not thunderstorms or high winds at sea also beautiful in their own way? Are they not harmoniously arranged taking their particular course? I think the reason why we sometimes fail to appreciate them is because of the accompanying danger or the fear of imaginary danger. If we, however, overcome this subjective element, we will recognise that the strong and violent processes in nature distinguish themselves from the peaceful ones only by the tempo of the occurring alterations. I can easily prove to you that irreversible processes, e.g. destructions, are not only common to explosive natural processes. They can just as well lead to the impression of rest and the

most beautiful peace. The only proviso is that an approximately station-
ary equilibrium of the entire action currents exists in and around the
natural structure, and that the destructions occur with a certain statistical
regularity. Thus the total character of the whole changes only evenly and
slowly, measured according to our standard.

Have a close look at the course of a brook or rivulet which meanders in
even bends through a peaceful valley. As you know, these bends are
changing constantly because of erosion, which is, of course, the cause of
their existence. The process of erosion, however, takes, a slow and regular
course only from the point of view of statistics. A closer investigation
shows that it is composed of an immense number of tiny and even tinier
catastrophes each time some small part of the bank caves in as a conse-
quence of having been hollowed out from below. And in the course of
events this leads to the death of a certain number of plants, apart from
the destruction of the "grown" soil structure.

The "complete harmony" which you see realised in the microworld of
every living organism is of the same kind as the one in inorganic nature.
The outer impression of "complete harmony" in the former is the result
of the principle of repetition, which governs the construction of organisms
and natural inorganic structures alike. That is to say, it is the fact that
every one of these structures is composed of similar, regularly arranged
components, which in their turn are divided into a number of the same
or similar elements down to the molecules and elementary particles,
which, after all, make up the whole. The organic individual as well can
only be formed and sustained, as the inorganic structure, by reason of
the intricate discrete action-currents which connect the whole with its
surroundings and its components with each other. Take, for example, the
action-currents which run between the various organs. To give some
examples: the hormones which are produced in some organs and in-
fluence other organs; the action of the heart and the nervo-vascular
system feeding the rest of the organs with the sustaining flow of blood
by regulating the circulation of the blood. Once again we find that
certain processes of destruction, recurring with statistical regularity, form
a necessary part of the apparently harmoniously proceeding course — for
example, the chemical digestion of food.

B All right, I will admit that. Nevertheless, there seems to me a much deeper
difference between the character of the inner harmony of, say, the land-
scape on the one hand and the living organism on the other. The difference
obviously lies in the fact that the particular kind of harmony which we
recognise in the appearance of every living being is the goal of a directed
striving of that living being.

The earth has a practically infinite variety of landscapes, which are all harmonious in their appearance and always beautiful in their way, provided they have not been spoiled by man.

On the other hand, living beings do not exist in an infinite variety of characteristics but only in certain clearly defined species. Between them there is no transition, except again where man interferes by cross-breeding. Each species represents, of course, a complete harmonious whole in itself, but as the goal of the individual striving is not expressed with the same perfection each time, the degree of harmony in the appearance of the separate individual is not always the same.

A Your very last observation is certainly correct but I would like to know what conclusions you are going to draw from it.

B It seems to me that this is the place where Plato's concept applies rather well. That is the concept of the eternal ideas which lie behind the objects of the world, which are, however, only imperfectly expressed by them. I think one can, in this sense, talk about the "idea of the species" whose duration, compared with the short life of the individual, is certainly eternal and which represents the perfection of the characteristics which do not appear quite perfect in the individual and only subject to individual contingencies.

Do not misunderstand me; I want to apply this approach only to living beings, possibly only to the higher forms of life. It does not seem to me to suit inorganic nature. Fixed, sharply distinguished types also exist in the world of micro-parts, but the separate parts belonging to one type do not have individuality from all we know, and cannot be distinguished from one another. Therefore they represent perfectly the general type to which they belong.

In macroscopic, inorganic nature, on the other hand, e.g. landscapes, one can distinguish very well types which are different in the particular cases by individual deviations and various degrees of perfection. However, in "macroscopic", inorganic nature each type changes in reality into its next similar type by hardly noticeable stages and one cannot help observing that there the classification into types is always somewhat arbitrary. It is of course out of the question to talk about the "striving" of landscapes to realise certain types. Nor can one say that of the various landscapes of, for example, upland country, one in particular is the most beautiful, thus representing the type of "uplands" in its purest form. This seems to me to be an essential difference between animate and inanimate nature.

A First of all, I think that the problem of beauty in the appearance of living beings is more complicated than your remarks have shown. However, to talk about it now would lead us too far away from our ethical theme. I am for the moment mainly interested in something else. Do your metaphysical inclinations really go as far as seeing metaphysical ideas in the platonic sense even in the division into species of living beings? Perhaps it is even your opinion that with regard to the striving of the organisms to realise their species type which you mentioned, it is a question of a teleological principle which cannot be explained by the laws of nature governing the inorganic world. Your recent remarks lead me to think so.

B   No, no, I want neither to reintroduce the platonic concept nor teleological assumptions which have surely become superfluous since Darwin. The concept of an "idea of the species" as I have proposed it just now needs no metaphysical assumptions. One can see it as the collection of all typical, general characteristics of species whose purely natural character is, of course, a fact for me also. I only referred to Plato because of my statement that, by comparison, these characteristics are eternal, and because of their property to form an harmonic whole. I think we do agree that any living organism is at bottom nothing else but a highly complicated servo-mechanism which has the same task as the man-made control-mechanism — that is, to maintain as accurately as possible a certain prescribed, desired state under changing external influences. I had this property of living beings in mind when I said that organic, stable structures distinguish themselves from inorganic ones by the fact that they do not, in general, suffer outer influences passively but react actively to them. I would therefore not see the goal-oriented reaction of living organisms at all as independent of the general laws of nature, but as a principle which is a result of them, as is the working principle of a man-made servo-mechanism. The great difference between the man-made control-device and the living organism is that the latter is actually building itself, although, in common with the former, according to a quite definite servo-mechanism programme which determines its development in the seed, and which is obviously a part of the idea of the species just as the characteristics are part of the prescribed, desired state that is to be maintained after development has been completed. It so happens that this idea is extremely complex and perhaps it cannot be described exhaustively any more than any actual organism. I am all the same convinced of the fact that it has nothing to do with metaphysics and constitutes nothing but an expression of the general laws of nature. Its particular form is defined solely by the special structure of the respective protein-molecules specific to the species. I expect you will not object to that.

I do not know, though. Do we not digress too far from our original ethical theme in considering such matters?

A   I have nothing against your interpretation of the concept of species if you see it in the way you have just demonstrated. My objection is about your opinion that we are digressing too much from our theme in considering such matters.

What would you say if I were to connect the value-oriented striving of man, and also the ethical striving, with the striving of the organism towards realisation of the prototype of the species, a concept which can be explained by general laws of nature?

B How am I to understand that? Do you seriously intend to conceive the ethical "must" as a part of the prescribed, desired state of the physical servo-mechanism "man"?

A And why not? All we have to do is to declare the idea "good" to be a component of the "idea of the species *homo sapiens*". This idea is, of course, not metaphysical but conceived purely scientifically in the way you have just demanded.

B Against that one can of course advance all the various fundamental objections which I have previously led into the field against any attempt to attack ethical problems scientifically.

Apart from that, the aim of the striving to realise the prototype of the species is, after all, a material one. It is the arrangement of all building materials of the body in a particular scheme. This we can take in the end as the spatial scheme of structure of the specific protein-molecule of the species and the spatial structure of the organ built on the basis of this molecule. The ethical striving, however, has a purely spiritual content.

A I might ask you now what you wish to be understood by the "purely spiritual". I suspect that a closer investigation of the concept will lead to an analogous result, as did our recent investigation into the question of whether scientific statements, e.g. mathematical ones, can be conceived correctly on a purely spiritual basis without reference to the existence and type of an objective, actual world. The result of that investigation was that there does not exist the "purely spiritual". In any case, it seems to me that it does not exist in the ethical striving, to use your own words. At the beginning of our discussion to-day you yourself stressed very strongly that in ethics particularly it is not only a question of the spiritual understanding of the problems to be investigated, but also the discovery of a rule for practical behaviour.

B The point in this case is obviously to bring the practical human behaviour, the various modes of behaviour of man, into relation with absolute values. These values, however, could very well be of a purely spiritual kind. However, let us put aside for the time being the question of the existence of the "purely spiritual" which I agree is somewhat problematical. I still cannot see how you can start with the scientific-biologically conceivable striving of organisms, including man, to realise a body structure defined according to species, and still arrive at a classification of the various human modes of behaviour which are in an essential degree not biological but sociological and have to be evaluated sociologically.

A Admittedly, we cannot do this immediately and in one step. We must first prepare the way for it. I propose that we should, to begin with, make a connection between the biological striving of all organisms to realise the prototype of the structure of their bodies with the modes of behaviour of animals in particular, disregarding, for the moment, all that concerns human behaviour and human ethics. When we have succeeded in this, we can later test wherein the behaviour of man differs from that of animals. In this way, I believe it will become clear which elements cause the appearance of social and ethical behaviour in man, and whether or not these elements can be understood on a purely biological, scientific basis.

B That will, of course, mean a postponement of the question which interests me most. But if you think that you can arrive at your solution in this way, I will agree.

Seventh Dialogue

The theme of the following discussion is animal behaviour and the problem of the development of the individual animal. However, it will not escape the attentive reader that practically all the questions which are broached stand in close relation with the fundamental problem of human ethics. At the beginning the discussion revolves around the question of whether the concept of "prototype of species" can be extended to the behaviour and mode of living of animals. A discounts all the reasons which B brings up against such a possibility. A also opposes the opinion of B that the anatomy of every individual is determined unequivocally by the hereditary material. He declares that the direction which the anatomical development of every individual takes is basically as much determined by environment as is his way of living. A particular mechanism regulates the achievement of an appropriate adaptation to the conditions of the environment existing at the time. As A words it, the effective prototype is defined by optimum adaptation as well as by hereditary characteristics. This prototype can be defined for the behaviour and the mode of life of the individual in exactly the same way as for its anatomy, and it can be considered as a "concept" in the same way as the prototype of the species. He states, furthermore, that, taken in this way, the prototype of the mode of life for many higher animals includes also complexes of characteristics which the animal instinctively strives to produce in its environment, animate or inanimate.

Finally, two points are discussed in detail. The case of two different instincts coming into conflict in certain natural situations of life, and the interplay of influences which sets in when a change of environment has instinctively been effected by the animal itself and releases new instincts.

B confines himself to critical objections on the whole, rather than, as in the previous dialogue, trying to lead the discussion himself.

A I think to begin with, we might start from the simple fact that each species of animal has not only a specific anatomy but also a mode of life characteristic to it which each individual tries to realise as well as the environment will allow.

B In other words, you want to juxtapose the prototype of the anatomy and the prototype of the mode of life, both conceived in an analogous fashion?

A Yes.

B But is not the mode of life of each animal, seen as a whole, already determined by its anatomy, while the individual mode of life, on the other hand, can be explained as a reaction to arbitrary influences from outside?

A Do you believe that such dependences could stop us from establishing a prototype of "behaviour" in particular and of mode of life in general?

B In some way, yes. In any case, they take away from this prototype the character of an independent quantity. The dependence of the mode of life on the anatomy, as the "independent" variable, is possibly not as disturbing as the dependence of the behaviour on the environment. I think we have agreed that the prototype of the species, with respect to the individual central device, plays the part of the preselected, desired state of the programme which it is the task of the regulator to fulfil independently of outside influences.

Where outside influences play a part there cannot be any question of a fixed regular programme, and hence also not of a prototype in the sense that we have had in mind.

That such a prototype is not effective is revealed also in the fact that one can hardly speak of harmony and beauty in the natural mode of life of the animal, at least not in the same sense as about their outward appearance.

A I hardly think your last remark is justified. We will probably have to speak later about the problem of beauty in the aesthetic sense. Surely, the same kind of harmony, and possibly beauty, as manifested in the anatomy of living beings can also be found in their natural way of life. I am talking of the uniform character of the whole which results from the regular repetition of equal or similar component elements, and the way such elements are assembled step by step out of renewed elements also similar to each other with the difference that the spatial juxtaposition is replaced by a juxtaposition in time. The change of night and day and the cycle of the seasons alone generate an appropriate repetition of certain time-linked events in the conduct of the life of most living beings. There are, however, as you know, sufficient inner periodicities in the course of the life of all organism as for instance hunger and satisfaction of hunger, sleeping and waking, tension and relaxation, rapid and decreased anatomical development and activity. If smaller or larger discontinuities, even catastrophes, are incorporated into this natural see-saw of every animal's life, yes, even if each life should begin and end with a catastrophe, it could only strengthen, not weaken, the analogy of the structure of the course of life of the living being, with its anatomy, as well as the structure of many natural phenomena which are felt by many of us to be harmonious.

Let us turn to the argument in which you suppose that it is inadmissible for a regulator to be dependent on the environment. Such dependent conditions caused you to reject the concept of a species-prototype of the mode of life. I think that you are, in this case, the victim of a misuse of concept as well as of a factual error. In the first place, the individual reactions of every regulator which has to effect a programme which is independent of the environment must, of course, depend on the environment if the regulator is to fulfil its task; for instance, it must react in opposite ways to opposite influences. You can observe that in any common temperature regulator. It reacts to a fall in the outside temperature by turning on or increasing the heating and vice versa to a temperature rise by decreasing or turning off the heating. Secondly, it is by no means at variance with an analogous definition of the regulator concept to allow even the preselected, desired state or regular programme itself to be dependent on the environment. Dependent conditions of this kind definitely occur in technical regulators. They are actually quite a general feature of the control device of living beings, and not only particular to the behaviour conditioned by the environment of animals.

B You are of course correct with the statement that the individual reactions of a regulator must necessarily depend on the environment. However, I do not know whether your last remark is correct. I mean, the remark in which you maintain that the regular programme for living beings is universally dependent on the environment.

We did start out from the prototype of the anatomy, which does certainly not display such a dependence on the environment. I have nothing against your extending the definition and taking other prototypes into consideration, which are dependent on environment as such. We should, however, in that case be clear about it that we are dealing with a new kind of control which is basically different.

A It seems to me that you create a conflict where there is none. Is the prototype of the anatomy of organisms really an absolute fact independent of the environment?

Let us consider the evolution of the species. We will find, on the contrary, a constant adaptation of the prototype of the species to the existing environment of the time. This is the exact opposite of the eternal and unchanging "idea" of Plato's, and I suspect that you are still under Plato's influence where your concept of the "idea of the species" is concerned.

B I have said that the "idea of the species" is eternal only in comparison with the lifetime of the individuals, and have of course no intention of denying the evolution of the species, which is a fact. Nevertheless, the prototype of the species does not change during the lifetime of the individual, and the individual cannot but reproduce it in a way fixed once and for all by the hereditary factors transmitted to him. Strictly speaking, the prototype of the species exists for the individual only by way of these hereditary factors. It is, so to say, only an individual prototype for the individual. We arrive at the general prototype of the species by finding the mean value of a great number of individuals —, that is, by way of an abstraction. Only the general type is found to be dependent on the environment in the process of evolution of the species, not the individual prototype which is alone effective for the individual, as the former must remain the same during the lifetime of the latter.

A I think you are mistaken when you assume that the anatomy of each individual is universally and always defined unequivocally by its hereditary factors. Does not the number of branches and leaves of a tree, indeed its entire shape, depend very much on the place where it grows, particularly on the incidence of light which guides its growth? Are not there even certain species of plants which develop according to habitat, in two separate types, quite different from each other, the dry type and the wet type, yet the hereditary factors are not different?

B Plants that have wet and dry types are the exception and therefore prove the rule, as the saying goes. It is true that the number of leaves and branches of trees and other plants of the same age depend also on the environment, but, on the other hand, the anatomy of the animal, more highly developed by comparison, is independent of the environment. For instance, the number and shape of the parts of the chitin or bone skeleton are absolutely fixed and do not depend on any influences of the environment, neither do number, shape and position of the muscles of each species, as you know.

A I don't think that the independence from the environment is as absolute as all that. It is, for instance, certainly feasible to influence quite considerably, especially in youth, the shape and size of muscles as well as certain characteristics of the skeleton by functional exercises and by the type of nutrition. I have never claimed that all anatomical characteristics of the individual can be influenced by the environment in the same way and to the same degree. All I wanted to do was to refute your opinion that the prototype of behaviour is different in principle from the prototype of anatomy, because dependence on environment is an indisputable feature of the behaviour of animals and, for that matter, of man, but let us talk about that later.

B And I maintain that in cases where the actual development of the anatomy is dependent on environment, it is not a question of the dependence of the individual working prototype, but simply a question of a more or less perfect development as a consequence of more or less favourable conditions of the environment which affect, in the particular case, the realisation of the prototype which is nonetheless purely hereditary. Whether we assume the prototype of the species to be general and abstract or concrete and individual, we find in any case that it cannot be represented perfectly by the individual. This imperfection is clearly an effect of the environment. With the exception of the really quite extraordinary species of plants producing separate wet and dry types, we could say that the actual appearance of an individual is all the more harmonious and beautiful with respect to the ideal of the species, whether conceived as an individual or in general, the more the actual environment approaches a particular ideal prototype of environment unequivocally defined for the species in question.

A This prototype of the environment you would necessarily have to define individually as well, so that the individual prototype can be realised in all its harmony, wouldn't you say?

B Exactly.

A I deny the idea that each individual living being has a prototype which is independent of the environment, but is completely harmonious in itself, and which is inequivocally defined by its hereditary matter and whose realisation can be only a little assisted or hindered by the environment. All we know points to the fact that the hereditary matter of the animate being is nothing but a mixture of the hereditary factors of the parents blended solely according to statistical laws, and therefore cannot possibly be harmonious. On the contrary, some of the hereditary factors must needs be antagonistic to one another. Accordingly, there can neither be a question of a uniform prototype, defined by heredity for the development of the individual, nor for an environment which is generally "favourable" or "unfavourable" to this development, since one and the same influence on the environment can be favourable to the development of one hereditary factor and unfavourable to that of another.

B Your words imply, to my mind, that you simply reject the concept of an harmonious prototype for the development of the individual. How, then, do you want to define this prototype other than by the hereditary matter which is undeniably a feature peculiar to the individual, without falling into mysticism?

A It is my opinion that such a prototype just cannot exist as a phenomenon independent of the environment. There is nothing mystical about it. We can simply define it as the optimum manifestation of the hereditary factors under the conditions of the environment existing at the time.

B And you credit the organism with the wonderful ability somehow to sense this optimum and to make it the goal of its aspirations? To accept this thought we have first to be able to form an idea of the way in which the organism could approach this optimum without us running into the danger of succumbing to the teleological concepts of the pre-Darwin type.

A I think we are not all that ignorant of the way which the organism takes to find the appropriate optimum solution. It is simply given by the fact that every organ and every separate factor develops according to the measure in which it can or must be exercised. That is how it happens that any factors which are less in demand under the conditions of the environment existing at the time are retarded in their development compared with other more useful ones.

B Then, it is your opinion that, in the course of the development of the individual, a selection takes place among the existing hereditary factors in the same way as among the various individuals during the evolution of the species?

A You could put it that way.

B There is but one considerable difference between these two processes. We are, ever since Darwin, well aware of the manner in which the selection takes place during the evolution of the species, yet we are essentially in the dark as far as concerns the mechanism of the selection of the hereditary factors at the evolution of the individual in spite of everything you just have pointed out. You trace it back to the fact that those parts of the body which are more extensively used are also better developed. But that does not explain anything as we do not know the direction of the development that is effected.

A It is true we do not know how the mechanism responsible for it works in detail. However, there is certainly no need for any mystical assumption for its explanation. At bottom, it is nothing but one of the forms of "learning" in the general sense. We have earlier mentioned it as a basic property of life. "Learning", generally speaking, is indubitably the acquisition of abilities. This acquisition always means a physico-chemical process which leads to constant organic changes, be it in the brain or in the rest of the nervous system, or in other parts of the body. Which abilities are to be, or have to be, acquired depends, of course, always on the environment.

My saying that the prototype of development of the individual is as dependent on the environment as the evolution of the species means nothing else than that not only the means for the achievement of a set goal can be learned but also the goal itself.

B I remember we talked about "learning" in connection with Pavlov's "conditioned reflexes". So far, I agree with you.

I think I can see what you are aiming at. I expect you are going, by and large, to apply your recent observations to the contemplation of the mode of life of animals; that is, you are going to define by analogy the disputed prototype of "mode of life" and "behaviour" of animals as the optimal realisation under the existing conditions of the environment of certain hereditary factors which produce a behaviour appropriate to the species. In this way you hope to overcome the obstacles which stand in the way of the prototype in question.

A Yes. I really am of the opinion that this way we can perceive that there is an all-embracing idea behind the behaviour of animals as there is one behind their anatomy. "Idea" is naturally to be taken in the strictly scientific, mathematical sense, without the slightest metaphysical tinge.

B I do see difficulties ahead. The hereditary factors producing a behaviour appropriate to the species are, I am sure, the reflexes and instincts of animals. However, these cannot be suppressed and are given once and for all to the animal and their aim is rigidly fixed. You would, however, have to assume instincts in which the degree of development would depend upon the environment and whose aims would be capable of being acquired in order to be able to apply your definition of a "prototype of behaviour" dependent upon the environment and to avoid the otherwise unavoidable interpretation of animal behaviour as a kind of purely mechanical translation of external impressions. No — please let me finish — I know you want to point out the Pavlovian reflexes. However, the animal does not acquire a new aim when it acquires them, but learns only how to reach an absolutely fixed goal in a new situation.
Besides, the animal is hardly ever conscious of the aim of the reflex action. I hardly see, therefore, in what sense one can speak of an acquisition of a new aim .

A You have not quite understood my reasoning. Under no circumstances do the hereditary factors depend on the environment as they are surely fixed at the moment of conception, but only the type and degree of realisation, e.g. in the case of instincts, the type and degree of the actual activity in practical life. The dependence on the environment resulting from that is precisely what we need in order to define a behaviour prototype analogous to the anatomy. It is, in that case, not at all necessary any more to assume a variable degree of development of the instincts irrepressible in themselves, which you mentioned. How does that strike you?

B Very well — that takes care of my first objection. I agree unreservedly. However, how about the question of ability to acquire new goals with respect to instinctive behaviour?

A I do not know, to begin with, in which way you intend to detect that the "aim" of the conditioned reflex is unalterable. You have repeatedly said that the common aim of all animal reflexes and instincts is to be found in the observance of a behaviour suitable for the preservation of the individual and the species. I would not say that this is correct in all cases, for instance, not for the atavistic reflexes, frequently peculiar to living beings, as you know, yet having already lost their original purpose. However, your interpretation would be appropriate for the greater part of animal instincts. Nevertheless, it seems clear that the behaviour suitable in this sense must turn out to be different in a different environment. This variability is doubtlessly achieved by the acquisition of conditioned reflexes!

Neither does your objection seem to be valid that the "learning" of unconscious aims is impossible. Consciousness has, after all, nothing to do with the general concept of learning inherent in the statement that new faculties are acquired according to environmental conditions. We had established that earlier, had we not? Of course, no animal knows the aim of a reflex action which it has executed in response to the stimulation of one of its senses. It may not even be aware of the action. Suppose a reflex-action has been caused by a stimulus *A*; after the animal has acquired a conditioned reflex the same reflex-action may be connected with stimulus *B*. In that case, the animal has undoubtedly acquired a new faculty and "learned" something. I expect you will agree. However, we must also take into consideration that, at least where higher animals are concerned, the animal is definitely aware of the aim of instinctive action.

B You mean to say that the broody hen, for instance, knows why she warms and guards her eggs and expects the hatching of the chick?

A That is just what I don't mean. But I would say that in other cases it has to all intents and purposes been proved that the direction of the instinctive action is towards a conscious aim which also depends to some extent on the environment.

B Please be kind enough to elucidate that by an example.

A We have discussed earlier the fact that mere sensation turns into perception of the objectively existing environment by way of forming conditioned reflexes through the coupling of stimuli of the senses which arise from one and the same object or set of real circumstances, and that in higher animals, instinctive actions, and even whole sequences of instinctive actions, are not occasioned any more by single sensations, but through the perception of certain concrete circumstances. It is but a small step to conclude that, in certain cases, it is not the actually perceived situation which serves as the stimulus, but imagined circumstances which are expected to be the consequence of instinctive actions.

Let us consider a complicated instinctive action — for instance, the building of an intricate nest or the digging of a warren according to a determined plan. The normal progress of these activities could be explained by simply assuming that each building stage releases the appropriate action, and we do not have to presume that the constructing animal has any idea of the finished structure aimed at, except in the very last building stage when an idea of the goal to be reached must exist. Without such an idea, which leads to the cessation of the reflex-mechanism when it coincides with the perception of what has been achieved, it could not be explained why the animal does not continue to build in the previous way once its habitation has assumed the right size and form. However, this idea could also come into action at an earlier stage, even before the building had been started. That arises, to my mind, out of the fact that many animals, which are quite capable of building for themselves, prefer to move into habitations deserted by animals of the same or even other species, instead of building for themselves. This would surely not be possible if the animal did not have, to begin with, an idea of the end result of its normal building activity. How else would it recognise that its find is suitable for its purpose?

B You may be right in what you say. Actually, however, you had promised not only to prove that imagined objective aims of instinctive actions of animals exist but also that these aims are dependent on the environment. In this respect the building of a nest as an example seems to me a poor choice. If your claim were correct that the aims of instincts are dependent on the environment, then the same bird would build different nests in different environments. Whereas the nests of all birds of the same species are the same in every place, they are even so similar that the initiated can deduct the species of the bird from the nest alone.

A No, indeed. No two robins' nests or swallows' nests are alike except in certain general characteristics, those which they must have according to the idea conditional to the species of the bird which has built it. On the other hand, they show many differences due to the degree of individuality of the bird and indeed of the environment. The bird can for instance only build with the material which it can find. This cannot be the same everywhere, but conforms only in certain characteristics. These are precisely those characteristics which correspond with the idea the bird has of the suitable material or else it would not be able to distinguish suitable from unsuitable material.

B If I understand you correctly you believe that not only a prototype exists for the general behaviour according to the species but quite a number of other distinct prototypes which also determine the bird's behaviour — for instance, a prototype for the suitable material that goes into building the nest which guides the bird when searching for material and finally also a prototype of the "nest as it ought to be".

A The complete prototype of the behaviour as well as the anatomy must evidently be of a complicated character. I have nothing against an attempt to stress certain partial prototypes governing certain sections of the behaviour. I have also nothing against the name "prototype" for such a complex of characteristics which marks certain exterior objects in the bird's mind, with the result that these complexes of characteristics give an aim to its behaviour. This is certainly the case both of the complexes of characteristics of "suitable building material" and of "the nest as it ought to be".

B Do you seriously believe a bird — to keep to our example — is capable of such a difficult process as selection requires? To be able to recognise in an object a certain characteristic or complex of characteristics one has to be able to select from all characteristics not belonging to this complex.

A I do not share your doubts. What do you understand by selection? Obviously only the neglect of all characteristics of the object but for one or a restricted number. This will not present any difficulty to the animal, for instance, in all cases where it does not notice any characteristics which it has to neglect. We find selection only difficult when we have to neglect all characteristics which have produced the concept of the object in a natural way and then must replace them by derived characteristics, accessible only at the price of great endeavour. This we must do for instance if we wish to describe a natural process in purely scientific terms or calculate it quantitatively or if we want to judge an event in daily life. Did you perhaps think of this process of scientific selection, which is indeed difficult to master, when you were talking about the difficulty in registering individual characteristics and complexes of characteristics?

B It hardly matters what examples one thinks of — selection remains selection. Without it individual characteristics just cannot be recognised as such.

A I think you overlook the fact that the animal may well be guided by certain abstract characteristics of its material environment as they are or could be without being in the least able to recognise the characteristics in their entirety, let alone give them a name, as is expected of the lawyer and the physicist.

B It may be customary nowadays to presume that animals are endowed with a certain ability of primitive thought.
I, however, have so far considered as a matter of course that thinking is simpler with actual real objects as operators, and that dealing with general characteristics comes later. But you seem to think differently.

A There is a simple scientific reason why thinking starts with the general and not the specific object. It is undeniable that thought can originate in sensation only. However, sensations are physico-chemical processes in the nervous system. They are subject to physico-chemical laws. As these are of a general character, it follows that the character of the sensations must necessarily be general. Blue of a certain spectral composition, say the colour of a clear March sky, evokes a well-defined sensation conforming with natural law. The same sensation, however, may also be evoked by a flower, possibly of a different spectral composition, provided the light it reflects excites the three colour receptors of our optic nerve in the same proportion — that is, provided the proportion of three energy integrals is characteristic for the sensation of the blue in question it does not matter from which specific object the light issues.

You agree?

B I expect you are right in this point. Having to admit that animals may conceive somewhat abstract characteristics of objects and even that instincts are directed towards such characteristics, it seems to me to take some power from your statement about the general dependence on the environment of the objective aims of instincts.

It seems to depend only on the definition of the concept we work with whether one arrives at one or the other result in respect of the existence of this dependence.

Calling, as you do, the real completed bird's nest, for instance, or the completed warren the aim of the building instinct you are of course correct in stating that this aim is dependent on the environment.

At bottom your last explanation, however, seems rather to imply that the actual aim of the building instincts does not lie in the finished nest or warren, but in the general characteristics of the structure to be built, but these are clearly fixed and independent of the environment just as the building instincts which essentially consist of them.

A I am sorry, I must contradict you. Experiments with animals have shown that, when unconditioned reflexes are connected with the perception of one objectively existing object, that is to say when a whole complex of stimuli acts as trigger, just some of the stimuli are generally sufficient to effect the reflex. The stimuli in that case do not have to have their origin in the object which used to act as a natural release. That is to say that a substitute object can take the place of the original reflex release if the substitute carries only a few of the characteristics of the original reflex release, provided that these are decisive in this connection. We will, therefore, not be very surprised that an environment which offers regularly the substitute but never the original stimulus release produces genuine conditioned reflexes now connected to stimuli belonging only to the substitute and not at all to the original stimulus release. Exactly the same can happen in respect of the characteristics supposed to be owned by an object which forms the aim of an instinctive action. One can observe these changes in quite a number of domestic animals, both the change-over from one instinct-releasing object to the other, and the change of part of the characteristics which are instrumental in releasing the instinct. Domestic animals do not only accept the housing and food surrogates which man offers them, they even prefer them. There are some blatant examples, however, that this change of habit is only conditioned by the environment and this is clearly shown in all those cases where domestic animals, when returned to their natural surroundings, turn wild and adopt completely the habits of their wild ancestors. Dogs, cats, horses and cows are well known to be able to do so.

B I am ready to agree that you may also be right in this. However, on balance I think that we have up to now not had much success in our discussion to-day. You have convinced me that the peculiar form of a prototype which is dependent on the environment is directing the development of every living being as you see it. The same form of prototype can also be considered as being decisive in the behaviour of animals, and that even the objective aims of certain animal instincts may change their characteristics under the influence of the environment. However, I frankly cannot understand how that can help us to comprehend the ethical problems of man.

A We had said that we would leave the human side alone for a while. We will have to consider some other points essential for the behaviour of animal before we can come back to man.

I am thinking above all of a phenomenon which I would like to call "conflict of instincts". You were once of the opinion that the impulses of animals, in common with virgin nature in general, form an harmonic whole which does not know any deeper inner tensions. I am not sure whether you still think so.

B I think I have said before that I have no objection regarding the use of your physical definition of the states of tension in stable structures and living beings as this is more or less obvious. I have also agreed that those states play a great part in animate nature. However, with regard to instincts, I must say I cannot yet see what these physical states have to do with conflicts between various forms of them. I have not changed my mind on this point, that is that only man knows real inner conflicts.

How can one expect impulses to come into conflict as they pursue the same aim, which is the preservation of the individual itself and the preservation of the species? Such a conflict could only arise if one impulse were to demand from the animal a reaction appropriate for this biological aim of existence and another instinct were to deny that same reaction — the dilemma of the inner conflict, however, comes about because man has not only impulses which correspond to the instincts of animals

77

but also impulses of a finer nature which are not subject to biological aims.

A   We will see later how it stands with the inner impulses of man which the animal does not own. In the meantime, I would like to consider your question regarding the connection between the conflicts of instincts and physical tensions. In the end, every instinct is directed to release a movement of a muscle. For muscles to move they must be brought into a state of physical tension. This is impossible without a corresponding state of tension in the appropriate motor nerves and in their beginning in the central nervous system. An instinctive motion must in fact be connected with the formation of a physical — possibly an electro-chemical — tension in the central nervous system. This tension will doubtlessly disappear after the execution of the reflex action demanded by the instinct, yet it must persist if the execution of the reflex is arrested, for instance because of a second contradictory impulse. At least the tension must remain as long as the external situation which released the first instinct remains unaltered.

B   And do such conflicts between two instincts come about?

A   Such conflicts can easily occur as a result of the dependence of reflexes and instincts on sense stimuli or particular objective characteristics of the environment. All that is needed is that a certain situation of the environment releases several sense stimuli or shows various characteristics at the same time, which engender reflexes and instincts which pull in different directions.

B   All right, I admit that in principle such a case is possible and can for instance easily be created in the laboratory. But it should occur only very rarely in the natural environment of the animal because, to fulfil their purpose, their instincts and reflexes must be adapted to this environment.

A   One can easily refute your opinion by some examples. Take for instance the animals of the African bush which is hardly touched by human hand. We know from many vivid tales that they regularly go to the watering place singly and in groups. Not only herbivores but also the beasts of prey. But what happens in a zebra, for instance, when, undoubtedly following its instinct, it goes to slake its thirst and perceives the presence of a lion, whose scent demands that it should flee according to another inherited instinct. Obviously a conflict must arise between the two instincts involved. The instinct to flee wins instantly because it is the stronger.

Do you imagine that the hen does not follow an instinct when she, full of fright, performs her peculiar, threatening dance in front of a dog to draw his attention from her chicks, most likely the same dance that her ancestors performed in a similar case in front of a fox or a wolf? And do you think that the instinct of self-preservation does not exist any more in such an animal? I should say that both instincts are there without doubt, but that the mother instinct proves to be the stronger of the two. Shall I give any more examples?

B That is not necessary — you have convinced me that conflicts of instincts occur naturally, even regularly in the life of animals. Nevertheless, I would like to say that these conflicts are conflicts more or less of chance and not of a fundamental nature like the conflict between the instincts of self-preservation and the demand of ethics which occasionally rend the inner man.

A What do you mean by "fundamental" nature of a conflict? I find that the conflict of instincts in animals, taken as a whole, is not of an accidental nature, because it is a definitely fundamental characteristic of real objects that they combine in themselves an abundance of characteristics and that they exert a variety of sense stimuli. It is also a fundamental characteristic of instincts and reflexes that they are connected primarily with single discrete sense stimuli or single discrete characteristics and complexes of characteristics of objects. It is a fundamental necessity that this leads to the said conflicts. Or are you of a different opinion?

B I have no cause to dispute what you say about the processes in the inner animal and I will not for the moment discuss the particular character of the human conflict occasioned by ethics. Yet I have my own opinions about that now as before. Before we come to that, I expect you will want to touch on some further points regarding the behaviour of animals — or do you consider that you have dealt with them already?

A No, there remains one point which is going to be particularly important for our discussion about human conditions. I mean the reaction feedback, to use a standard technical expression. That is the fact that the control mechanism "animal", dependent on the environment not only in its separate actions but even in its regular programme, reacts on the environment even as it fulfils its regular programme, frequently to quite a considerable degree.

B I see you have again the home-building activity in mind. In the case of its daily routine and on behalf of its young the animal does indeed first create a certain environment. This in its turn gives rise to certain reflexes by characteristics which have been created by the animal itself. We have discussed this interchange quite thoroughly earlier on.

A Yes, the home-building activity belongs of course to the chapter, but not alone. I am thinking for instance of the fact that every animal forms part of the environment for other animals, just as they form part of its environment. The result is an interplay of action and reaction between the individual and the part of its environment which consists of other animals of the species — a "reaction between control input and control output", just as in the case of nest-building.

B   However, that can hold only for gregarious animals.

A   It holds for them in a larger measure, but it holds for others too. Don't you think that the sex life of animals proceeds along the same lines of mutual release of reflexes?

B   Taken like that I think one might also find that similar reactions occur quite frequently between animals of different species as well, for instance, when beasts of prey attack their victim. In that case too the actions of one releases reflexes in the other and these in their turn lead to certain reactions of the former.

A   Certainly — but for us the most important are the mutual relations between gregarious animals of the same species because they always have relations with each other not only during the time of reproduction and when raising the young. In these we can frequently observe an interesting division of tasks executed by individual members of the community for the good of the whole.

B   You are thinking for instance of the division of labour and reproduction by bees and ants.

A   No, not at the moment. The different functions mentioned are decided in bees and ants by their difference in anatomical structure, so that there is no possibility for one individual to take over the function of the other. I had in mind mammals and birds which live in societies in which various distinct functions fall to some animals — for instance, the function of leader or look-out who has to give warning of the approaching enemy. Every adult animal is, in this case, fundamentally capable of fulfilling each of these functions. It can change from one function to the other or need not carry out any if all necessary functions are already fulfilled by other animals.

B   Why do you think that this circumstance is of particular interest for us?

A   Because it seems to me that there we have to deal with the same kind of objective target as we have found in the construction of the habitation. We find that, in that case, the most varied reflexes come into action according to the external situation. These have only one thing in common. They are all aiming at the realisation of the prototype of the nest appropriate for the species. It means that the electro-chemical tensions necessary for the release of reflex actions do not occur if the prototype to be realised by them has been found to have already been realised.

By analogy, I imagine that every member of say a herd of antelopes or wild cattle has an inherited image of the "herd, as it should be" containing certain functions which have to be fulfilled. Provided the functions are fulfilled by one or other member of the herd according to the prototype of the herd organisation none of the other animals experiences the impulse which would drive it to occupy the position in question. Should a position become vacant every one of the rest of the animals will feel the urge, more or less according to its position in the herd, to step in the position itself and so help to realise the prototype of the herd once more.

B If your assumptions about the character of the prototypes guiding the endeavour of living beings is correct, it would mean that the prototype of the organisation of the various animal societies just mentioned is dependent on the environment.

A It is that without doubt. I think this is best shown by the domestic animal. Only those can really be domesticated which live gregariously because of their natural inclination to do so. In their consciousness man takes the place of the leader animal. For that reason we find that, for instance, dogs or horses can be obedient to their masters out of their own free will. It even gives them pleasure to do so, as does the satisfaction of any natural impulse. However, there can be no question of a voluntary subjection of animals whose wild ancestors lived solitary lives and which have therefore no community instincts beyond the sexual one.

B You mean the dog considers his master as a sort of "leader-dog" and the horse feels he is a kind of "leader-stallion".

A That is not only my opinion but the opinion of most, if not all, animal psychologists, who are concerned with this matter. The state of affairs is, in this matter, the same as in all other impulses which are orientated towards some concrete object marked by certain complexes of characteristics, or which are released by such an object. We have seen earlier that it needs only some of the characteristics to arouse the appropriate instinct.

According to all we know, the most important characteristic of a herd-leader is strength and intelligence if it is to be recognised as leader by the other animals of its community. It is therefore quite natural that animals with community instincts subject themselves gladly to man if he only shows them that he has all these important qualities. It does not matter in that case that he lacks many characteristics peculiar to the leader animal of the species. On the other hand, we find it quite often that the subjection and the attached obedience are refused regularly if the man who assumes the part of master is not able to show his superiority to the animal in a manner that it can understand.

B By the way, the sphere of action of the herd instinct is by some animals in their natural environment extended to members of another species, as shown in the mixed herds of the African bush.

A I do not know whether the connection between for instance Zebra and Gnu is as close as between Zebra and Zebra. However, a certain mutual relation cannot be doubted, at least where warning of the approaching enemy is concerned.

Eighth Dialogue

B *defends the opinion that the difference between man and animals is that man does not only share their inner impulses, which can be explained biologically and which depend on the environment, but he has also incentives of a finer and absolute kind. B sees in this the true root of human ethics and all civilisation.*

A *on the other hand, points out that such a dualistic interpretation of the processes in the inner man can hardly be sustained. Contrary to B, he sees the roots of human civilisation in precisely the fact that all human impulses are dependent upon the environment, particularly those that have the changing of environment as their goal. He sees the roots also in the enormously increased ability of man (compared with animals) to influence the material environment, and in language which has made it possible to hand down from generation to generation the highly variable contents of consciousness. The approach allows also the explanation of the special phenomena which show in the historic change of morals.*

At first B does not see how the actually given inner logic of the development of civilisation can be explained in this way. He believes, furthermore, that A's point of view does not permit the proof of the necessity of the ethical primacy of society over the individual. He attacks with several arguments when it becomes clear that A's point of view is the Marxist thesis that ideals are fundamentally dependent on material circumstances. The reader must draw his own conclusions about who is right after following the course of the discussion.

A I think we are now ready to turn to our next point and to investigate the fundamental differences between human and animal behaviour.

B I must make a preliminary remark to this straight away.

A Please do.

B It is connected with my criticism of Kant. I have said before that I do not believe that the ethically good deed must necessarily, nor even in preference, be the result of maxims. I want to extend this statement to all human actions. I do not believe that the entire human behaviour is different from that of the animal because in the end it is guided by intelligence and not by instinct. As we both have frequently said, logical, intellectual activity can fundamentally do no more than base one argument on another argument. In the present case, the last argument can be nothing other than an inner urge which must remain unfounded and which is unfounded in principle. There is no other way to convince somebody that an action or inhibition of an action is necessary except by showing him that the action or its inhibition is demanded by the undeniable inner urges which he may be expected to have. The argument is without avail if one is mistaken in that expectation. To give a rough example: to be threatened with death is no deterrent for somebody who, for some reason, does not fear death any more, nor can he be tempted with pecuniary gain if he does not desire money.

Arguments of general value can exist in practice only in so far as they rely on inner urges which may be expected to exist in every human breast, and are capable of being assumed *a priori* without any argument. Don't you think it is so too?

A Yes, I share your opinion. It seems to me, nevertheless, that an essential difference between man and the animal lies in the decisive part which intelligent argument plays in spite of all. We have observed in animals that certain inner impulses are not released directly by sense stimuli, but by being related to more or less abstract objective characteristics of objective facts. In man, we find these objectively dependent impulses have a majority over those which represent a direct reaction to simple sense stimuli. Furthermore, predominant amongst the former are those in which the abstract characteristics to which they are bound cannot even be reduced any longer directly to a complex of simple sense stimuli, whereas this is most likely always possible in the animal.

The effectiveness of such a human impulse presupposes a fairly complicated intellectual activity as it would not be possible to ascertain without it the existence of the characteristic in question with which it is connected.

B You may be right. However, we would understand each other better if you could show by an example what kind of impulses you have in mind.

A There is no difficulty in giving such an example. Think of what importance the wish to earn money assumes for many people, and of the mental energy that is expended in analysing the environment to find the one characteristic which denotes whether the environment affords a chance of profit or not. This characteristic is undoubtedly not represented by a complex of sense stimuli, and to recognise it one must have the gift of combination and the ability to think in objective relationships and not only sensory relationships, all of which goes far beyond the mental faculties of any animal.

B I willingly admit that many people show a great deal of perspicacity and ingenuity in earning money, and that this requires a certain mental attainment of which animals are not at all capable. Neither are all humans capable of it to the same degree — I for one am practically incapable of it. However, I do not know whether the wish to earn money can really be considered to be an original instinct in the same sense in which we undoubtedly must consider animal instincts.

Maybe quite a number of original instincts hide behind the greed for money — for instance, the urge to be somebody, the lust for power, the general urge to influence as much as possible one's environment, which is always easiest for people with money as our social conditions are. Greed for money, however, can hardly be an original instinct, for it can only occur in a civilised environment where money is used.

A What do you mean by original instinct in this connection? We can, after all, recognise instincts only by the very characteristics by which they are released, or whose production is the aim of the instinct. Even when discussing animals, we have observed that the environmental characteristics which define a particular instinct can be of a very complex kind, and their very composition may even depend on the environment itself so that one cannot define the said instincts independently of the environment. Where animals are concerned, there may be some sense in distinguishing between an "original" and a "derived" form of the instincts, the former being the form which is more or less rigidly fixed in the natural environment of the animal, and the latter being the form which is adapted in a changed environment — for instance, in the state of domestication. On what, however, do you mean to base the distinction in the case of man? Man could not survive in an environment which is not modified by the use of tools and arms. The form in which human drives are supposed to appear in a primeval environment is therefore fictitious, and we would be wise to occupy ourselves above all with forms which exist in reality. It could, all the same, be of great interest to investigate how, and according to which laws, these forms react to changes in external conditions, in particular to changes in the degree of civilisation of the environment.

B I gather anew from all you have just said that you consider all drives of man to be dependent on the environment in the same way that the instincts of animals undoubtedly are. Perhaps you deny altogether that man has any drives which the animal has not, and which are basically different from animal instincts.

A I do believe, indeed, that the human heart knows drives which are unknown to animals, whether in its natural environment or when domesticated. But I consider even these specifically human drives to have developed genetically from animal instincts and that there is no basic difference between them.

B This is just the point I wanted to draw attention to with my remark. I have no intention of denying that reasonable argument plays a much greater part in human action than for animals, and particularly in the manifestation of drives which are dependent on the environment. Yet I would say that a much more essential difference between man and animal is that man has drives of a finer kind, apart from instincts which are basically the same as those of animals, and which can be interpreted as having developed in the course of environmental influences and genetic evolution. These drives can hardly be open to such an interpretation. They differ from animal instincts not only because their objective is non-biological, but also because they are of an absolute character and do not depend upon external circumstances. They can therefore be considered original in the same sense.

A You know our opinions differ on that as we have discussed this point repeatedly.

B Yet to deny as you do the finer drives would, to my mind, take away the only firm prop of the individual in practical life, and rock the very foundations of human society.

Mulling it over, I find that our preceding discussion has in this sense only strengthened my conviction of the non-biological character of the fundamental ethical phenomenon. The alpha and omega of all your explanation is that all biological objectives are dependent on the environment without exception. You have even succeeded in showing me this dependence in places where I had not suspected it up to now. However, the more it becomes apparent that any biological impulse is conditional on the environment, the less suitable it becomes to form the foundation of the true ethical principle.

A Closer inspection shows that when you speak of the independence of the surroundings of the ethical demand you speak of something that ought to be demanded itself so that ethics can fulfil the purpose you ascribe to it.

I think we really ought to prove first the existence of such impulses of a finer kind whose aims are really independent of the environment and which can be distinguished from impulses which have a biological foundation and which are dependent on the environment. — In this connection I would like to ask you a concrete question. To which category of impulses do you count love between the sexes which is at bottom surely a part of the general sexual pattern of nature? You won't deny on the other hand that in love, particularly, is revealed — maybe not always but sometimes — the most sublime and undoubtedly specifically human impulse.

B I don't deny it at all, and I admit that it would be a very subtle biological task to distinguish the biological elements from those which really are of a sublime, purely human character. Yet I do not consider that such a division is impossible in principle. It is assumed that there exists love between the sexes, which is sublimated and free from all eroticism, that is, in it the finer elements are in practice separated from the baser ones. I am forced to admit, however, that I personally have not yet come across such love, nor have I been able to observe it in others. I cannot deny that this constitutes a certain difficulty with regard to my concept of things.

A And what do you think of mother love? Do you think one could in its case also separate the "finer" from the "lower" elements?

B In principle I expect the position is the same as in the case of love between the sexes. Both impulse- complexes are doubtlessly connected with each other.

A To which category would you allot the impulse which can, in case of danger, cause a mother to risk her own life to save that of her children? To the lower impulses, which can be explained biologically or the finer ethical ones? I must point out to you that in the latter case the animal must also be endowed with "finer" impulses, which you declare different in principle from the various other impulses.
To avoid misunderstanding: at the moment we are not interested in the question as to whether man is endowed with inner impulses which the animal does not know. I quite agree that he is, but we are interested in the question as to whether all that appears to be "finer", worth while and "good" in man in the ethical sense is fundamentally foreign to all nature outside man.

B To answer first your question regarding the characterisation of the motive concerned with the self-sacrifice of the mother, it is quite in accordance with my concept to assume that the animal reaction in such a case is explained purely by impulses which can be explained biologically, but that the reaction of the human mother also contains, over and above these, impulses of a finer kind, depending on her general ethical level.

A You mean, it would be possible that these "finer" impulses might also be lacking in the soul of the human mother and that, in that case, her sacrifice would not be evaluated as ethically positive?

B Yes, just as, for instance, sexual intercourse without participation of the finer forces of the soul.

A We are both of the opinion that even purely impulsive actions could be considered good in the ethical sense. And now you wish to except from the start the possibility that the acting impulses in such a case could be of the kind which the animals own as well.

B I think I might consider this possibility for the case of mother love which you mentioned. However, I know that the problem is of fundamental importance and I would in that case have to revise my standpoint regarding the entire ethical question. Furthermore, the examples of sexual and mother love have, as essential components, impulses which are closely related to animal instincts and have doubtlessly been genetically developed from them, and I think they are perhaps least appropriate to explain the question in which we are interested. Other human impulses and impulse complexes exist, which as a whole are widely separated from animal instincts and are not at all open to a biological approach.

Think, for instance, of the scholar who has dedicated all his powers to pure knowledge and who — not a rare case — gambles with his health, yes, even his life, for this finer purpose! Assume, if you wish, that occasionally thirst for glory plays a decisive part, although I don't think that is very probable as the execution of scientific work means surely the most tedious and also most uncertain way to glory. Yet you must admit that ambition, independent of its doubtful ethical value, is something specifically human, only possible within the framework of human civilisation.

A   A kind of social order of precedence exists also among gregarious animals, so does a very clearly pronounced desire of the separate animal to acquire a better position in this order and certainly not to lose the position once having gained it. I would say that the impulse responsible for this is related by way of evolution to human ambition, however different the civilised state in which man has to find his goal might be from the swarm or the herd of animals.

B   All right, I concede that. However, I have said that I doubt if ambition is the determining factor among the impulses of the scholar. I am sure his happiest moment is not when he emerges with a new discovery and is applauded but when he has the first flash of knowledge sitting alone behind his writing desk or when he and his closest colleagues find that the successful experiment makes the inspired guess a certainty.

You cannot really claim that the animal kingdom knows anything vaguely like science, nor would you say that any animal has the urge to acquire pure knowledge, this urge being free from all direct, as it were material, interest in the object of research. For us the satisfaction of this urge means the greatest bliss.

A   Science is, of course, unknown in the animal kingdom. Yet the urge for pure knowledge exists even there, in exactly the same primitive form as in the human infant. You also may have indulged in the horrid game of pulling out one leg after the other from long-legged beetles and spiders until they cannot move any more from the spot. If you have done so, you will also remember that the motive of the game was not cruelty and pleasure in torturing, but plain thirst for knowledge, the wish to understand the mechanics of running.

B   I cannot really remember having indulged in the activity you describe.

However, I know it is frequent in children of a certain age. I also agree with your interpretation of the motive.

A   You know, the same game in all its phases has been observed in chimpanzees living free in the virgin forest. I am not talking of animals in captivity where human influence might have spoiled them.

B   I find that most surprising. Should that really be the case, then I must admit that the simple urge for pure knowledge would not be a convincing example for the existence of impulses in man which cannot be explained biologically. Well, I am not going to doubt the veracity of your statement, nor am I going to say that the psychological reasons for the game must necessarily be different in monkey and man.

Let us leave examples for the moment. I would really like to know now your answer to a much more general question. Do you actually still recognise a difference in principle as well as in degree between man and animals? If so, what makes the difference in your opinion, if it is not the finer motive that cannot be truly evaluated biologically, the existence of which has been for me the reason for this difference?

A   Before I answer that, I must make it clear what we intend to understand by "in principle" and "in degree". As I have said before, I see between man and animal, as every-where else in nature, only gradual transitions and jumps of the same type as they occur also in cases where man is not concerned. It is not only your opinion but also mine that the significant difference between man and animals is man's ability to create and carry on civilisation.

However, I do not suspect finer, purely spiritual, irrational or whatever other mystical forces as the cause of this ability. I see it as the result of a development which has taken place according to absolutely rational laws which are well known, and which continue to take place. It is my opinion that there are only two biological basic requirements for the creation and preservation of civilisation. They are related with each other and when they exist they are sufficient for the actual occurrence of civilisation. One prerequisite is the ability to influence the environment which we have found also in animals, but which man has to an enormously increased degree. In our recent discussion about the living organism as a control mechanism we have classified this ability as "feedback of the output to the input". The other is language.

B   Of which beginnings can be found in the animal kingdom!

A   Yes and no. The "language" of animals is at a stage of development which lacks one essential factor, namely the ability to express an infinite variety of subjects, old and new. This ability is a decisive factor with respect to the measure of influence on the environment. Closely connected with this ability is the characteristic of the human language not to consist of speech symbols which are inherited and therefore *a priori* rigid, but of speech symbols which are virtually arbitrary and which have to be learned according to circumstances.

Where animals are concerned, communication is limited to a fixed number of subjects equal to the fixed inherited number of symbols, these being a standard part of the characteristics of the species. Subjects and symbols of communication can therefore only increase in the course of the biological development of the species, whereas the human languages, as you know, undergo constant changes and progress rapidly. Anyway, the individual symbols are not, as in animal language, the decisive factor in human language but the fundamental categories of concepts largely common to all human languages. It is the pattern of thought, general and eminently adaptable, which forms the nucleus of all language, the essence of the various speech symbols. It is the system of thinking in statements and questions, or orders, or wishes; the pattern of subject, object, attribute and verb, of past, present and future, singular and plural, etc. All these categories are expressly represented by prefix, suffix, changes of sound or special words or by the order of words, not to mention others. The general application and hence adaptability to new subjects of these thought-categories is a necessary condition for the rapid development, as compared with the development of the species, of civilisation or, if you like, various human civilisations.

B Do you mean to say that the existence of language as well as the increased ability to influence materially the environment, suffices to create a civilisation which does not concern itself with material aims and subjects only? It is, of course, obvious that a civilisation is not feasible without a language to enable each generation to hand on its experience and knowledge in readily digested form, that is, without a language that is able to adapt itself to unforeseen and changing contingencies. But to make use of the possibilities inherent in the language, and for civilisation really to begin and continue developing, I am sure there must exist another driving force.

A And to what do you ascribe this driving force?

B I couldn't tell you — but I would assume that forces of a non-biological character are engaged so that the same biological stage can be accompanied by widely different stages and kinds of civilisation. If the factors determining the development of civilisation were of a biological nature, one would have to be able to trace specific biological changes responsible for the changes in civilisation.

A ... Which constitutes for you a new argument to attribute the origin of civilisation to factors which are not to be grasped by reason, and which are mystical in the last analysis.

B Possibly.

A I quite agree with your opinion that the pertinent conditions which cause changes in civilisation while biological factors remain the same cannot be of a purely biological nature. Accordingly, I do not believe that the opinions and laws arrived at by the study of animate nature other than human are sufficient for the understanding of the development of human civilisation. That does not say that the origin of civilisation has to lie on a "higher" level which is not attainable by strict observation and rational explanation. I think the driving force that you are looking for behind the development of civilisation lies simply in the special character of the feed-back — and for feed-back read influence — on the environment which distinguishes the human control mechanism from that of animals. We know from the theory of servo-mechanism that the result of feed-back can vary considerably according to strength, sign and type. It can, for instance, lead to the regulator continuing in a specific state or the slowing down or speeding up, increasing or decreasing of the oscillation in this state or a permanent or possibly continually increasing change of state in a definite direction or even to the superimposition of several such processes.

All these forms can be recognised quite clearly in the development of human civilisation except perhaps the first form. In this, a state once reached is continued with stability. This is really contrary to the nature of human civilisation, whereas such continual stability or, at best, oscillation around a given point, is typical for the control mechanism of animals. The operations which animals perform on the environment may be quite considerable; we have only to think of the beaver dam. Yet they have all one thing in common. They start from the original, given state of the environment, taking always the direction and continuing only for the set distance characteristic for the species in question so that the impulse exerted by the new environment is fixed from the beginning. It is in the animal world that the interplay between influence of the environment and the reaction of the organism on the environment is prescribed to the last detail. The interplay determines the prototype of the mode of life, which is more or less sufficiently defined by purely biological factors. The moment, however, when, as in the case of man, any possible direction and dimension of influence on the environment can occur, the interplay of action and reaction between organism and environment may take on a quite unforeseen character. The only assumption necessary is that human impulses, like those of animals, themselves depend on the environment with respect to the objects that release them or form their goal.

B You are saying that the reason for the difference between man and animals is this: the animal is forced into the same predestined mode of life by the entirety of its inner impulses. Man, however, makes his way outside such once and for all prescribed routes by the circumstances of civilisation created by himself because these in your opinion, once created, change the direction of the impulses that have led to their creation. This then repeats itself with each activity of the impulses once they are deflected from their original path. To use a simile: compared with the biological time-scale the development of civilisation is exceedingly precipitated. You see it like an avalanche opening on its way down new sources of energy which speed up its rapid descent.

A   The analogy of the avalanche is appropriate in so far as it concerns the opening up of new sources of energy for the continuation of the process once it is started. Apart from that, however, it is not a very happy choice. The avalanche is after all essentially destructive — civilisation, on the other hand, constructive and positive.

B   Does that not show the fundamental weakness of your theory, being able to explain the negative but not the positive side? You have always doubted the validity of my opinion that a consideration of civilisation along purely biological lines can only lead to a negative evaluation of cultural phenomena, and that it cannot do justice to its positive ideas. The various expressions, concurrent as well as consecutive, of one and the same civilisation may have certain inner contradictions, yet you cannot deny that, seen as a whole, they have an unmistakable logical connection.

A   I do not know why you think that my roughly sketched outline of the development of civilisation must necessarily lead to a chaotic process.
On the contrary, the scientific interpretation of the human impulses makes it much more probable that various expressions of civilisation arising from these impulses show at least the same harmonic connection as the manifestations of life arising out of the fundamentally homogenous impulses of animals in their natural surroundings. This connection is of the same kind as the connection governing the anatomy of the animal or any complex whatever of animate and inanimate objects of nature which form islands of interaction in which the discrete "paths of reaction" exert continually similar influences on similar parts. This yields doubtlessly part of what you have just called the inner logic of the development within the realm of civilisation notwithstanding certain inner contradictions. These have their natural parallel in the instinct conflicts of the animal and finally in the unavoidable tensions of all macroscopic, organic and inorganic, material, natural phenomena.
You can say more. In each civilisation certain human impulses stand for essential paths of reaction. We have already seen that certain impulses

can, in animals, be directed towards the achievement of a complex of abstract characteristics in the environment. You have yourself in this connection spoken of, for instance, the prototype of nest characteristics of a definite species of bird, such a prototype being defined by abstract characteristics, and you might as well have used the word idea to describe the sum of the abstract characteristics in question. After all, they contribute to the definition of the prototype of behaviour in its entirety and constitute thus a part of the idea of the species, to use your own expression. Let us simply allow the human impulses which are directed towards the creation of civilisation to have the same quality, i.e. that of being directed towards the achievement of certain complexes of abstract characteristics in the environment. This would explain that the various manifestations of one and the same civilisation are governed by certain general complexes of characteristics. In other words, it explains the logical connection between the various manifestations precisely through the principles of the interpretation which you attacked.

B However, this logical connection is obviously interrupted when you assume that the general characteristics which form the aim of the striving for civilisation are themselves not fixed but change in more or less arbitrary fashion dependent on external conditions.

A But why should these changes come about in an arbitrary way? We have seen that the dependence on the environment of all instincts in animals is decided strictly according to rule. That includes, of course, also all instincts whose aim it is to influence the environment. The dependence on environment is the result of the fact that regular shifts of accentuation are possible inside complexes of characteristics, the actual occurrence of which leads to the release of an instinct, or its realisation forms the aim of the instinct. The shift in accent achieving the result that various individual characteristics of the complex may take the place of the whole complex. In this way the various objects to which the instinct can be attached remain always interconnected by certain common characteristics. That does not mean to say that the same, common characteristic must belong to all objects of the series. Furthermore, a certain characteristic may be common to only some of the objects in the series.

True, we have seen that, through the formation of conditioned reflexes, new characteristics may enter the complex of characteristics in question. However, these new characteristics cannot appear at random because their occurrence is conditional on the general laws of nature governing the material environment of the animal. If we assume that dependence of human impulses follows some analogous law there can be no question of random occurrence.

B What you say may be more or less appropriate for the material side of human civilisation. Experience shows that satisfaction of any human need immediately creates new needs. This process really does seem to be the reason for the material development of civilisation and it is possible that it differs fundamentally from the corresponding process in the animal kingdom which does not lead to civilisation only because, as you say, direction and size of the human influence on the environment are not strictly determined beforehand. All the same, to be honest, it is not clear to me how you intend to explain with this scheme the development of the ideal content of civilisation unless you intend to declare yourself a follower of the Marxist theory of the development of civilisation. This theory, as you know, states that the ideal content of civilisation is determined by its social structure, and its social structure is determined by the ability of man to influence materially his environment.

A And what have you against this mode of explanation?

B It appears to me, to put it mildly, somewhat too one-sided. I do not deny that there is always a certain dependence of the ideal civilisation on its material foundations. I think it goes too far, however, to see in this dependence the only determining factor. After all, there are human aspirations that do not depend on material conditions. I do return again to the trinity of values of our first discussion — "Truth", "Beauty", and "Goodness". I am convinced that in the last instance they can only be measured in absolute values, even if it is very troublesome really to find such standards. We have discussed this point at length, particularly with respect to ethical values, without having reached a final solution. With the Marxist theory of development of civilisation it works out that the course of material usefulness is not only a contributory factor but the deciding factor for the course of the evolution of mankind.

A I think with this opinion you are under a misapprehension. I am sure there cannot be anybody who would seriously undertake to deny the rôle of purely spiritual aspirations for the development of civilisation. I, for one, would not attempt to do so. The absolute standards for ideal values is quite another question. Agreed that each social order and every possible civilisation in it must surely recognise the trinity of values you have mentioned and give it pride of place in the ideal Pantheon. That does not say that the criteria for what is declared true, good and beautiful have to be always the same. I would even say the criteria must necessarily depend on the material conditions of life at the time of the representative epoch.

B And how do you mean to prove this opinion?

A I would suggest treating the problem of beauty at a later date.
   We have already discussed truth in detail. We are, I think, agreed that reality exists independent of the recognising subject. Neither of us doubts,

therefore, that the concept of truth acquires meaning when defined as agreement between idea or statement on the one hand and reality on the other. Because all knowledge has the character of a model, the agreement can take place in isolated points only, and not as a whole (otherwise the brain model which lies at the bottom of all knowledge of the object would have to be identical with the object). That is the reason why such great variations are possible about the content of true statements about a given object. Which statements can be made depends without doubt essentially on the material conditions of observation. The development of our present knowledge of physics, for instance, would have been quite impossible without the contemporary development of technical aids for the corresponding observation and without the, by former standards, grandiose industrial plants for the manufacture of these aids. On the other hand, our enormous technical possibilities may lead us astray to pursue solely knowledge that can be proved quantitatively and to neglect sources of knowledge that need no particular technical devices to be tapped. Truth remains truth, but which truth can be discovered and which truth seems worth the search depends clearly for the greater part immediately on the technical means of research that are available. I do not know if you have any objections to that.

B   No, not as yet. Do continue.

A   Not quite so simple is the question with respect to ethical values. You will, however, in any case, agree with me as well if I say that ethical problems have, in the first instance, a social character.

B   I have pointed out this circumstance in particular more than once.

A   Any social organisation can exist only on the foundation of certain material conditions. For instance, the constitution of the medieval town rested on the guilds and trade, the feudal system and bondage on agriculture. The modern freedom of movement and formal equality of the citizen were enforced by the needs of industrialisation, and did not owe their realisation to the mere philanthropy of the powers that were. All those are admitted facts about which we need not argue perhaps any more than about the fact that the raising of herds was the reason for primitive nomadism and the change to husbandry the reason for the first permanent settlements.

B   This leaves the field wide open for all kinds of different questions. However, the fundamental fact that there is a definite relationship between the type of social organisation and the way in which people earn their material living seems indisputable. I also think that there is no point in discussing these things any further.

The essential point for us lies somewhere else — that is, in the question as to whether the social function of the ethical standard must necessarily have as a consequence the dependence of the standard on the social form of the time. I would think that such a conclusion is not at all justified. If you want to convince me you have to bring up other arguments. The social function of ethics especially seems to me to represent a particular difficulty for your attempt to solve the ethical question. Leaning on my suggestion to call the entirety of typical characteristics in animals and plants the idea of the species, you have recently expressed yourself to the idea of the species homo sapiens — that is, as that part of the idea of the species which supplies the prototype for the behaviour. You have disputed my theory according to which the hereditary substance given to each individual constitutes quite generally the prototype peculiar to that individual, which it must necessarily strive to realise. You were able to convince me that for various reasons such a prototype can only be determined as the optimum realisation for the given circumstances of the hereditary substance.

That does, however, in no way deprive the definition of the prototype of its individuality. Even for creatures of the same species in a given environment the optimum realisation must always vary as they have different individual substances. If we therefore intend to base the idea of good on the biological prototype of human behaviour, we are going to obtain an ethic which is, right from the beginning, not social but individual in principle. The aim of all aims is, after all, one's own personality which it is necessary to develop to the optimum.

A I think you are confusing individuality with egoism — that is, the possibility of variations of the ethical demand for different individuals with the general content of this demand. The latter could have a social character in spite of the variations in all individuals. Man is, without doubt, biologically a social creature. Having found that, in social animals, the idea of the species is often represented by the prototype of the herd or pack or swarm which determines the behaviour of the individual decisively, there is no reason why we should not suppose, by analogy, that man has an inborn idea of the typically human society as it should be, which demands of him to act above all as a part of the society and not as an individual.

Granted that this inborn idea does not only depend on the environment but is, in various respects, subject to individual changes, for instance, inasmuch as it allots various rôles in the society to the individual according to his gifts. However, that does not have to impair the essentially social character of the ethical ideals. Nor does it have to lead to an egoistic ethic, with the aim of a principally individual nature in which the interest is above all in the development of one's own personality as you suggested.

B Splendid — I am glad that our opinions coincide concerning the ethical superiority of society over the interests of the individual. However, I still do not believe that the natural social urge to which you refer suffices as a foundation for human society. Suppose the overall structure of the ideal human society shows large individual variations in the minds of its members? In that case, individual persons, each endeavouring to realise their own idea of society, would have to quarrel. The result would be that no individual idea could succeed. Yet we have to assume these variations if we ascribe the existence of these ideas to biologically inherited factors.

In fact, man has succeeded in creating a social order. This suggests the conclusion that another principle must be active, a higher principle which does not depend on subjective factors. Generally, individuals submit to its superiority. If they do not temporarily, it leads invariably to dissolution in public morals also. History has shown that time and again.

A We must also assume that the prototype of the herd shows individual variations of the idea held by separate members of the herd, and nevertheless the herd is truly realised, yet we never assume that animals must be guided by a higher unifying principle, in order to be able to understand that.

B Of course, the primitive urge to imitate helps making each animal do as his neighbour does.

A You think that this urge to imitate does not function in man?

B I have no intention of denying it. I just do not believe that it suffices to unify the diverging human tendencies in human society the structure of which is so much more complicated.

A The urge to imitate does not have to suffice. After all, the universal means of communication, language, is not only capable of disseminating the knowledge of the technical device for changing the environment, but also the ideas themselves according to which the change of the environment is to proceed. It is therefore impossible in human society that the individual should develop any idea in complete individual seclusion without being influenced by the action that guides his contemporaries. That does not, of course, exclude the possibility that in one and the same society contradictory ideas can be developed running parallel to each other.

By and large, however, the reciprocated influence of ideas of different individuals is going to have an equalising tendency. In any case, no idea active in the community is going to be determined by purely individual factors and is going to direct the actions of one individual only. That is also, needless to say, valid for the ideas that determine the image of the community as it ought to be in the minds of its members.

B All right, I agree that communication by language leads to an approxima-
tion of the ideas which guide the separate members of society. All the
same, I do not think that touches on the crux of the matter. If the mechan-
ism of the development of civilisation were really to function as you
describe it, one could not understand why times occur, in the develop-
ment of civilisation, where regression takes place even in the realm of
morals.

However, if one contemplates the development of civilisation as a battle
between higher and lower principles, regression has its own explana-
tion, that at times the lower urges of man get the upper hand.

A You understand by "lower" urges the immediate biological ones which
connect man with the rest of animate nature?

B Fundamentally, yes. I concede to you, as I have said, that the actual
differentiation between the "higher" and the "lower" in man's breast is,
in many cases, a problem difficult to solve. We have been exercised on these
points earlier on. In any case, I do not yet understand how you mean
to explain the phenomena of degeneration and decay in the development
of civilisation from your point of view if you do not recognise a difference
in principle between higher impulses that create civilisation and impulses
that can be explained entirely biologically and are really inimical to
civilisation. Or do you intend to explain cultural and moral decay as
symptoms of illness, and ascribe them, like physical illness, to the action
of external influence of disturbances, which act as pathogenic agents?

A Yes and no. Indeed, the corruption of morals which we can observe
frequently in history is regularly a complex affair in the creation of which
quite varied external causes can be active. But there is no necessity for
special external pathogenic agents. The tension between morals as they
should be and morals as they really are may also be a result of the fact that
the ethic ideal lags behind the external circumstances on which it must
depend like all other human ideas, according to my opinion. This tension
must even be perpetual, not only in times of crises. It is only more
obvious in the latter. We have already observed in the animal kingdom
that conditioned reflexes are acquired after a time lag. It requires a
certain exercise before the reflex becomes automatic and, on the other
hand, it takes time to forget it. What is valid for conditioned reflexes
coupled to simple sense impulses is surely also valid for the more com-
plicated psychological processes that replace an object to which impulses
refer by an "ersatz" object. I think this is quite an important property
of the formation of reflexes. If the mentioned time lag did not exist, any
single accidental external occurrence would disturb the reflex mechanism
of the animal. Whereas, as things are, single incidental sequences of
sensations, providing they are not too violent, have no influence and

corresponding accidental alterations of environment leave no mark. Only such impulses which mean a lasting change in the course of the accustomed lines of reaction produce a permanent reorientation in the mechanism of reflexes.

Man also is endowed with this insurance by time lag, and it is surely as useful to him as to the animal. A side effect of this is that man's mechanism of impulses seen as a whole always lags behind the progress of the civilised environment; the more it does so the faster the progress is.

But that is not all. The ideas at the realisation of which certain complexes of impulses aim are never the purely private property of any man. They always have their roots in the general fund of ideas of the general society, bound together by the language or, as you might say, the social consciousness. The content of the social consciousness will always be determined, to a much smaller measure, by the comparatively sparse new ideas newly created in the midst of the contemporary generation than by the richer fund of ideas handed down by the past generations.

It takes, of course, much longer to adapt this to the alterations of the environment than it does for the first-mentioned purely biological factors.

B What you say is actually not new, as Goethe's Mephisto says in the famous quotation,

>Reason turns to nonsense, good deeds become a curse,
>
>Woe to you that you are a descendent.

However, unless I am very wrong, that refers to the phenomenon of senility in the courts of justice of the society and not to moral concepts. They belong to a much deeper layer of civilisation difficult to be got at, and may be exempted from the relativity that rules other cultural phenomena.

A If you take, like me, morals to be a phenomenon of civilisation, you must admit that they are subject to the general time lag between the culturally dependent contents of consciousness and the material development of civilisation.

B I must tell you that your last statement which infers that ideas are generally and unexceptionally dependent on the material environment seems even less plausible to me than in its specific application to morals. It seems to me to show a lack of sense to maintain that the material conditions of civilisation are always in advance of the ideas when you consider that these conditions owe their existence to the ideas. And that is what your statement comes at, if you consider it as generally valid.

A Of course ideas which aim at the creation of certain material conditions must precede those particular conditions. The achievement of these conditions will generally take some time. But then, I have not been claiming that any ideas lag behind those material conditions whose realisation is the goal. However, in fact every idea whose content is directed towards the change of reality has another relation to reality in the fact that, in its turn, it is dependent on the material conditions existing before its conception, to a large extent — in fact, for the biological and social reasons we have discussed.

B Of course you are right. I admit that the general train of thought of yours is logical in itself on this point and is not shaken by my objections. However, I do not consider that the moral question has yet been clarified by your remarks.

Ninth Dialogue

In this dialogue the two participants discuss mainly, to begin with, the question of the ethical evaluation of various inner urges. Later on, they concern themselves with the relationships of the separate individual and his private ethics with the state of civilisation of the time of society as a whole. B wants to believe that human qualities exist which are always virtues independent of the state of civilisation of the time and others which must always be considered sins according to his beliefs of the existence of two fundamentally different types of inner urges. He is inclined to consider the development of these qualities to be independent of history and essentially determined by individual factors. He would rather not recognise a social code of honour as the moral regulator for the individual.

The discussion turns, furthermore, on questions of conscience, of professional honour and of class-free society as well as the humanitarian ideal of Christianity and its connection with Christian ethics.

A has opportunity to expound his opinions about the dependence of the moral ideas and possibilities of the individual on the fund of ideas and material conditions of life of society as a whole. He also enlarges on the kind and extent of influence of the individual on society. He does not think the possession of fixed, ethical attributes by certain human impulses is possible.

The opponents agree, to begin with, really only on one point. They reject any kind of life-denying ethics, although A can express this denial only conditionally, owing to his fundamental views.

A You intended to make certain objections to my claim that moral ideas depend on material conditions of life.

B My objections are quite simple. You must agree that certain virtues have always and at all times positive moral values — for example, honesty, industry, public spirit and conscientiousness. Whereas other properties — for instance, dishonesty, unreliability, laziness, selfishness and negligence — have always a negative character and will always remain so whatever material conditions of life and social system prevail at the time. It seems to me that in their case, the rules usually governing the decay by time of ideas of civilisation do not apply.

A Well, I do not think that, for instance, industry and conscientiousness have always had the same moral value which they undoubtedly have to-day. Nor do I know whether they will keep their importance in future. I suspect that, in primitive times, courage and powers of decision were comparably much more essential to the general moral image of the man. So much so that a lack of some of the positive properties you mention had no weight at all — for example, industry and conscientiousness.

B It seems to me that courage and powers of decision signify surpassing moral strength in our present state of civilisation as well, although I did not mention them earlier on. I had no intention of giving a full list of all morally positive properties of man.

A Do you really think that an all-inclusive list could be made?

B No, I do not think so. For the reason that I, unlike you, do not believe the ethical phenomena to be sufficiently conceived by reason.

A I think that a complete list of all properties of ethically positive value is pointless because the ethic ideal is, by nature, a unity which implies more than can be achieved by the enumeration of all parts. In any case, only a comprehensive conception is possible if, as I propose to do, one intends to conceive the ethical ideal as the optimum realisation of the goals of inborn urges in their entirety. This way, the ethical ideal acquires the character of being completely determined rationally, yet is never actually analysed in every detail, in the same manner as the character of the ideal physical function of the organism or the prototype of its material construction. After all, we know by experience that every increase in one moral quality results in a decrease of a different moral quality. Whether the decrease means it is insufficient and therefore the increase that it is too much depends entirely on the circumstances. We know that in the comprehensive image of ethics certain human qualities and actions acquire importance again and again at different times and under different conditions. That is to say that their existence is required in a particular measure. The only reason for this can be that certain qualities in the social structure and in the material foundations of society repeat themselves. Their existence stresses these particular points when posing the moral problem for each individual.

B I will readily concede that the moral stress on the various positively valued qualities can be different at different times and under different circumstances.
However, it still does not make sense to me that the ethical ideal should be orientated towards the sum total of urges comprehending every urge in existence. In this connection every urge must have the same value. I do not intend to champion an ascetic philosophy, but would not think it advisable to include in the sum total of urges necessary to fulfil the ethical problem any urges that connect man directly with the animal kingdom — for example, the urge for food and the sex urge. I am fully

aware that the sexual urge in particular has been considered divine, for instance in the ancient religions of Asia Minor, and accordingly received a positive ethical evaluation. Yet the morals and manners of the times, when such was the case, were of a kind which we can only consider to be human aberrations. Similarly, we know that in primitive times of civilisation the need for sustenance assumed divine affinity in the shape of the harvest goddess. Even less appropriate do I consider it to give the same value to urges which are really in themselves immoral like avarice, envy, and jealousy, as to magnanimity, gratitude, or the impulse which urges man to apply himself with all his powers to the interests of the community.

A When you talk of some urges being inherently immoral, you forget that all inner impulses which we can in effect observe in ourselves are not only released directly or indirectly by external impressions, but have also been affected by the environment. They cannot appear in the same form in another environment. They have always positive or negative value with respect to the environment in which they appear, according to whether they direct towards or deflect from the goal of the ethical ideals in the given circumstances. Neither is your statement correct that all inner urges have the same value with respect to the realisation of the ethical ideal, according to my exposition of the ethical problem. The avarice you speak of must clearly be an impulse belonging to a definite social structure in which private ownership of money plays a great part. The word avarice is used with respect to this urge only when it has acquired an undoubtedly negative character because of its one-sidedness and violence. It is the same with envy and jealousy, which do not exist as abstract urges, but only with respect to certain conditions of environment. They acquire the names mentioned when they signify an ambition that is of negative value, ethically speaking.

The same, but with the opposite sign, is applicable to the evaluation of such inner urges as gratitude, magnanimity and the urge which drives man to apply himself to goals which lie outside his own narrow interests. Speaking of the satisfaction of the sexual impulse and the need for sustenance, the entire human civilisation would not exist if our ancestors had not obeyed these urges constantly. To declare them inferior seems to me nonsensical. That does not exclude the possibility that their satisfaction could become immoral under certain circumstances which might occur with varying frequency. In the same way could certain urges which you count among the impulses of higher nature become immoral. The comprehensive definition of the ethical ideals, the only one possible to my mind, excludes any distribution of fixed ethical attributes to urges independently of the circumstances of their field of action in the same way as it forbids a moral assessment of action according to abstract characteristics selected at random without reference to the whole. The juridical evaluation of human actions is of course a different matter, but does not really concern us in this context.

B   Don't you think that your considerations must lead to a different evaluation of the various components of man's inner life because you start from the scientific biological basis? We are aware, of course, nowadays, that, genetically, man has evolved from the animal. And does it not follow that everything that distinguishes man from animal belongs to a higher level of development and is therefore to be considered of higher value?

A   This can certainly not be claimed in such general terms. There are certain features of the human anatomy which indicate a level of anatomical development already surpassed by various higher animals. For instance, the multiplicity of toes and fingers of man used to be characteristic for the ancestors of all present solipeds whose species have developed beyond the level on which man has remained. An analogy for inner impulses might exist, although I cannot name any example. In any case, the concept of a biological level of evolution only makes sense within the line of development of one and the same physum. It can hardly be applied to the qualities of the human soul in particular because we know as little about the inner life of our primitive and pre-human ancestors as about that of our distant descendants.

B   I don't think it is as hopeless as all that to try and find a biological basis of evaluation. I am thinking of the fact that, based on certain results of comparative phrenology, one is able to make certain statements about the question as to which parts of the human brain may be considered to have completed their phylogenetic development, and which are in a state of incomplete biological development. One believes that one is able to say that those parts of the brain assumed to be the carriers of intellect have experienced their complete phylogenetic development, but not those parts in which the social and emotional qualities are located.

A   The gist of your contribution is this: certain spiritual qualities of man, particularly important from the ethical point of view, have not yet completed their biological development. Presumably the type of behaviour which is going to be considered good after an appropriate lapse of time of further development — always presuming that the human race is going to experience this development — is going to differ from the present type of behaviour even if we neglect the fact that the environment of man will have changed considerably, and if we imagine the carriers of the various inner urges exposed to the same arbitrary environment. Yet the type and laws of human thought are presumably going to remain essentially the same.

104

Yet neither the inner life of our antecedents nor that of our descendants can determine what is good and what is bad in an ethical sense, but only our own heart. I therefore think that it is not a rare case for the genetically older impulses to give us the direction to act positively in the ethical sense, while younger impulses work against it. The reverse may equally take place as well as a common direction of impulses of different biological age.

B The impulses we feel directly are certainly more or less dependent on the individual as far as they can be explained biologically, and are based on animal instincts. Do you not believe in something like a conscience which serves as a signpost for honest actions and which is independent of individual limitations?

A I certainly do. As we have said before, the ideas which govern the consciousness of man cannot be his private property, for the consciousness of each individual must mirror essentially the public consciousness of the society to which he belongs since he constantly exchanges ideas with his environment. That must of course also be valid for moral ideas, and I think that the word conscience means nothing else but the sum total of the moral ideas of the society active in the individual.

B This statement of yours really does not do the individual enough justice. If it were true, the conscience, according to its content, would be determined from outside, and there could no more be a question of the moral superiority of an individual. The individual, apart from the exceptional genius, will not be able to exert an influence on the content of the social fund of ideas. If he were to take that as the highest authority he would have to give, in principle, the final decision on his action into the hands of others. Rather than that I would still believe in the moral superiority of man following the inner voice which calls him towards good and is, in essence, unconditional and not dependent on the individual. It is my opinion that he is only morally beholden to this voice, and not to society. In any case, I think that your view robs the conscience of its independent function, which is its essential character. It seems inconsistent of you to base the determination of good on the sum total of impulses which are active in the inner man, but yet let the conscience, as the actual guiding principle for ethical actions, be determined by factors which approach the carrier of the conscience from outside.

A I think you did not understand me correctly. Why should the conscience not be able to act directly from wherever its content stems? I am quite of your opinion. It is everyone's own problem to grapple with one's conscience. I also think that man is responsible only to himself with regard to morals.

Nevertheless, it seems to me that the natural idea of society as it should be includes from the start the actions of its members along the lines of the moral ideas which govern the society. These determine what we call the social "honour" of the individual. I am sure you too will acknowledge the social dependence of the ethical ideal accomplished in this way. Or do you wish to extend the moral superiority of the individual to such a length that there is no room for the concept of honour as the moral respect which the individual enjoys in the eyes of the community?

B To be honest, I must admit that I do not think much of the concept of honour in general. Remembering the concept of academic professional honour in our fathers' times and partly also in the times of our own youth, I can only welcome the oblivion, at least to the younger generation, into which the academic code of honour has sunk with its aberrations in the field of morals which did nothing but encourage hypocrisy.

A I think you are letting out the baby with the bathwater. It is true that, in the past, honour took usually the form of professional or class-bound honour. This is, however, because society in the past was based on the existence of classes which was a condition of the material foundation of human civilisation in the past. That the class code of honour led to abuses happened because, in the meantime, the society built on classes of different social position had lost its material foundations and its entire justification. However, that does not necessarily condemn the social code of honour altogether. In a class-free society it will be free of the abuses which you and I find so repulsive.

B What you say is nothing but a repetition of a former chain of thought of yours applied to a particular case. Nevertheless, I wish you would explain more precisely your view of the limitation of the ideal by the material. I also am convinced that the achievement of a class-free society — if it is possible at all — would lift the human existence onto a higher level than we have to-day. However, up to now, I have always considered that the class-free civilised society, and its ensuing freedom from injustice, has been an unattainable ideal valid for all times and not only for the present epoch, and independent of any material preconditions.

A That is not an ideal but a utopia.

B Yes, perhaps.

A I think that the conquest of the class society and the connected injustice could remain utopian only so long as the technical possibilities of mankind were limited. While the state of technical aids is low the production of the immediate necessities of life requires so much labour that he who is engaged in it has no time and strength to work on higher problems, i.e. for the creation of works of art and scientific research.
High civilisations, in former times, could only develop on the basis of a labouring class, which freed a much smaller class from the labour and

worry of producing their own means of existence, leaving them free to create and develop civilisation. Their results served as a justification for the class system without which these results could never be attained. However, the justification exists no more, considering the present state of technical aids which are at the disposal of mankind.

B You mean that, if present-day technical aids are properly used, all mankind would be able to participate in the achievement of civilisation, if not in the same manner, doubtlessly to the same extent?

A Yes.

B If that is your opinion, and you may be right, your chain of thought would lead to the concrete conclusion that it is a moral duty to-day to change most of the social and political systems in existence, at least as long as they are in the way of the creation of such a state.

A I am indeed of the opinion that any social and political system, or part of such systems, which hampers a currently possible social progress has thereby lost any justification that it might formerly have had and its elimination has therefore become a moral duty. Man is, seen purely biologically, foremost a social creature; i.e. the social idea which he has to realise has by nature pride of place in that part of the idea of the species which governs actions. The moral prevalence of social habits is even increased under conditions of civilisation which do not allow any expression of life of man which is not determined socially, and I think therefore that it becomes the most essential moral duty for any civilised man to work for the creation or preservation of the best possible form of society of the time.

B Don't you think that an individual could live a moral life without definite social direction of activity, or without particular political interests as long as he fulfils his duties towards his nearest and dearest? After all, the ability to influence society is practically nil for people who do not have a particular prominent public position.

A On the contrary, it seems to me that no man can live under civilised conditions in any case without exercising social influence in the true sense, i.e. actions through which he influences for his part the whole of the general development of society. We do not only act by our own actions but also by those by which we voluntarily or involuntarily induce others to act. Talking earlier of the moral duty to work for possible improvements in the social system, I was not thinking only of a particular social activity which is especially directed to this goal. I thought of the fact that everybody who is guided in his actions by certain general ideas — as we all are — either strengthens or weakens irrefutably the public strength of the ideas, their power over other people, by the way in which he realises these ideas. Let us consider the question of professional honour which you yourself have broached earlier. Do you not think that everybody, living as a member of a class, contributes either to the decline or on the other hand to the preservation and improvement of the general idea, the expression of which is the behaviour suitable to one's station, by the way in which he complies with the demands of the honour of his class in his most personal and private behaviour?

B I think you are probably right with that statement.

A All actions of all members of a civilised society are dependent on each other. They are connected by an interlacing of actions with each other, which corresponds entirely with the causal connection according to the principle of discrete actions in nature. Even he who keeps away on purpose from any social activity would exercise all the same intensive negative or positive social reactions. His moral, or immoral, mode of life could in no case be considered to be his private affair.

On the other hand, I also believe that the moral state of the society or class of society to which he belongs limits the possibility of every individual of leading a moral life because of the moral influence of his contemporaries from which he can never quite escape. To put it more precisely, it is limited by the ratio of the actual state of the society to the state which would portray the optimum realisation of the general human ideas of society under the given conditions.

B Your last words prove once more my suspicion that there is not enough room in your conceptions for the moral superiority of the individual. The conclusion to your statement is that the moral individual is largely drowned in the sea of society and admits in effect of no initiative on behalf of the individual, so to say.

A But why? You have agreed yourself just now that every man is in a position to strengthen or weaken the power of certain ideas which guide the society to which he belongs by his own actual behaviour. Yet one more point must be added. We must not forget that the public fund of ideas including the moral part surely never represents a static self-contained whole. Rather, the fund of ideas is developing constantly. It is ever in a state of transition which is marked by conflicts of varying vehemence between old and new components of ideas. The individual is therefore at liberty to decide between the two spheres of ideas with which he comes into contact as a free and sovereign agent and on his own initiative, even if he is not capable of making a new contribution to the public fund of ideas. What he cannot do is to contribute all on his own without the help of others.

B You do not see, therefore, the inspiration of genius which is given to privileged humans as a kind of illumination as from heaven without reference to the fund of ideas of the environment.

A I am, as you know, convinced that no human idea can be conceived without reference to the material and ideal conditions at the time of conception.

B Well, I also think that the development process of ideas can only be conceived historically. The only quarrel is with the degree of influence of material factors possible on the events in the realm of ideas. You have, however, been able to convince me that this influence does take place. Yet, you cannot deny that the creation of ideas and the consequent general development of society progresses often by leaps and bounds. It also frequently seems to be tied to the intervention of single eminent personalities, which seem accidental from the point of view of this development.

The immense, almost magical, influence, surpassing by far all usual proportions, which such personalities effect gives rise to the thought that in such cases exceptional forces are at play that are not usually normal in the life of the society.

A The influence of individuals of this calibre appears extraordinary only if one tries to consider the development of the human society divorced from all knowledge of science. Nature is, as we know nowadays, contrary to ancient belief, full of discontinuities. We also know quite well how these discontinuities occur. In macroscopic structures at least they are, as far as we can see, bound to the existence of stable compound structures which are capable of standing tensions but which are destroyed when the tension becomes too large. Social institutions of economic, political or moral character have similar properties of stability. They may be under pressure because they have lagged behind the development of the given material circumstances. When a large section of the community feels that their existence is a burden it does not require a particularly great effort to release a powerful irreversible reaction. The effort may well be within the power of one man. This occurs quite analogously in nature with respect to material structures which are already under tension.

B You are probably right. But please tell me, how, do you think, does the genius differ from ordinary men? Or do you simply deny the appearance of a genius as a singular exception?

A I think life poses a number of problems to every man. They may be quite personal or they may actively involve a certain number of contemporaries; they may be problems of professional, of family, or of general human types. The individual solves these problems more or less completely or he may not solve them at all. The problems he has to deal with are, however, always similar to those that assail people in similar circumstances.

I would say we use the word genius simply for people who succeed in solving a problem typical of its kind and decisively important for the community. They succeed in solving it before any one else is able to and in a manner which is acceptable to others.

B What are the conditions which create such a prime solution? Don't you think that singular personal conditions are always necessary?

A Of course, the person whose performances we feel are brilliant must always have definite special gifts which correspond with the demand of the problem in question as well as industry, perseverance, courage and steadfastness, and last but not least, certain external lucky circumstances without which the brilliant performance would not have been realised either. It is certain, however, that factors of some exceptional type play no part. By exceptional factors I mean that the majority of men do not come into contact with them, that they lie outside the usual composition of things.

B I think one can agree with this concept as well.

I do once again want to return to something that was said earlier on. We have talked of certain general virtues which are deemed necessary for the realisation of the sum total of the ethical demand, as far as we can see at all times, although the stress may vary. We also agreed that, in civilised circumstances, social ideas are particularly prominent ethically. You also are of the following opinion which I am inclined to dispute. Your opinion is that the individual ethical demand depends always on the circumstances of civilisation of the time, and that the actually unvarying parts, which you do not deny, are only a consequence of the existence of characteristics of civilisation which are also, in fact, unvarying.

A Correct.

B If that is so, then variable components of environment which exist without doubt must correspond with certain variable components of the ethical demand. In particular, special ethical demands must arise in the present which have validity at no other time. I would like to know whether you can name such a special ethical demand.

A We both agree, if for very different reasons, that the ethical total demand evades a comprehensive rational definition. You do not expect my answer to be complete, do you?

B No, no, I have only asked you to name any ethical demands whatever which are characteristic for the present only.

A I have really answered your question at the time when we talked about the concept of class-bound honour. A moral ideal, human in the widest sense, which ignored the then existing class system would have become a destructive factor as far as civilisation was concerned if one had seriously tried to realise it in a society where the burden of civilisation rested on the shoulders of the small cultured section of the community. The latter could only exist by material exploitation of the numerous serving class. Nowadays, of course, this ideal of humanitarianism in the widest sense is the only valid one as the realisation of the class-free society has become a moral duty.

B   I too consider the proclamation of the moral ideal of special and quite general human qualities to be necessary. Its introduction must really have quite far-reaching reactions. I could be satisfied with your answer and the reasons you give for it if there were not a few objections of a fundamental nature which we have not yet touched on in our discussion.

A   I would like to discuss these objections with you, but first allow me to make two more remarks regarding the questions you have asked me. The first concerns the active character of the ethical ideal. This I consider the only possible one to-day. It is my opinion that no kind of negation of life, philosophy of renunciation or fatalism, can be permissible for modern man whether in regard to his private life or the life of the society. In particular. I think that the immense possibilities in our power of affecting the environment and ourselves impose a social duty on us. We may not consider social injustice or cruelty to the individual as the inescapable fate which it is our moral duty to suffer passively. The possibility of influencing the material environment has given to the hand of humanity a lever which allows it to achieve fundamentally any result not only physical but ideal as well as social. It is our duty to help with the achievement of such results if it means moral progress.

To press my point, I think that for us to-day it has become impossible to escape ethically into contemplation, which shuts an eye to difficulties and circumvents them instead of eradicating them.

B   Just what I think — I even carry my deduction further. I believe that a passive philosophy has been, and is, reprehensible under any circumstances, whereas you think that only nowadays must our philosophy be active in principle. Do you really believe that abnegation of life could ever have had an ethically positive character? Before you answer that, let me say something more on this point. I have hinted earlier that I am no adherent of Christian philosophy. There are several points that repel me in Christianity. The first is the ultimate importance of the individual in the Christian philosophy. Although preaching thou shalt love thy neighbour, it proclaims as the ultimate aim of actions the achievement of one's own bliss. It is striking that the actual social effect of preaching love has been very small in the highly civilised western countries during all the years of Christian domination. It has never really been able to make far-reaching social improvements, not even to enforce the discontinuation of the most flagrant abuses. One should really have expected better of a religion which has love as the central image, except that love is a means for a different purpose. Furthermore, I think that there is a second even more essential reason for the actual social impotence of the Christian renunciation of the world. One cannot seriously, and with all one's powers, strive for the improvement of one's neighbour's circumstances if one renounces life in general and looks for the goal and real completion of the human life only after it is ended in the hereafter. I therefore would like to ask you specifically: do you consider that Christianity and Christian philosophy could ever be really considered justified owing to the fundamental renunciation of life?

A Let me answer your general question first. I do believe that there are times when the inclination to contemplate and seek your treasures in the hereafter, while suffering unalterable external circumstances, can be of a fundamentally positive character.

Furthermore, I think you have overlooked one essential point in your judgement of Christianity which conquered a world which had come to a dead end through the fall of the antique civilisation. You are certainly right when you say that Christian philosophy is egocentric in the last resort, and must therefore be considered antisocial. You are also correct in your statement that the principle of charity is largely ineffective socially. I think, like you, that Christian charity is fundamentally no socially constructive principle, not least because of its connection with the renunciation of life and the world.

This renunciation of life is, however, historically necessary with respect to the general humanitarian character of the Christian ideal. Christian teaching considers man as man irrespective of class, at least according to the four gospels. Yet a purely humanitarian ideal could not appear other than detached from the world and profoundly unconcerned about the conditions in life in the framework of a civilisation that could not exist without classes owing to insufficient technical aids.

Otherwise its result would have been detrimental to civilisation. Let me express it this way. Christianity had to pay with unworldliness for the premature concept of an ideal which could not be put into practice at the time and for a long time to come.

B I find this is an interesting thought. Given than your opinion is correct — and I support it — that it is possible now to realise the class-free society, one may draw the conclusion that Christianity, while retaining the ideal classless man, may be freed from blemish of unworldliness. It is possible that to-day the transition from an inner to an active Christianity is considered to be a duty.

112

A You mean, to put it bluntly, that it would be possible to-day to found something like a Christian Marxism?

B If you like to call it that, yes! Anyway I have the notion of an association of the humanitarian Christian ideal with profound social reforms.

A I cannot believe in the success of any attempt to free Christianity from its unworldliness and rejection of life while keeping its other essential content and so enable it to perform penetrating social changes.

B And why not?

A The pretension of Christianity to preach unalterable eternal truth is much too static to achieve really drastic reforms. Any theory, and particularly any philosophy, must be fundamentally dynamic if its aim is to achieve radical changes in the state of the world not only once but again and again. A doctrine of revelation like Christianity that cannot be corrected by experience is doomed from the beginning quite fundamentally to unworldliness and to far-reaching practical ineffectiveness, if it is true that new cultural situations demand always new ideologies, which conviction is the necessary consequence of my approach.
It is not one point of Christianity but its entire essential content that must be turned inside out to eradicate this fault.

B I could say something more about that. However, I do not feel called upon to defend the Christian ideology. I suggest we continue the discussion we started about the particular ethical demand of the present.

A I would like to dwell on another point which seems essential to me. It is also connected with the enormous growth of our technical means. I am thinking of the present-day centralisation of economic activity. The nature of our present-day technical means demands the increasing concentration and consolidation of places of production, working separately in former times, without which the technical aids may often be useless. We find, therefore, that everywhere in the world, where modern techniques penetrate, a concentration of enormous powers of production in unified economic organisations takes place. This course of development is itself a condition of the nature of technical progress and can therefore not be stopped.
My intention is to point out the moral effects of this phenomenon. It means the end of the social position of a great number of persons who had been independent in a preceding period of economics and their transition into a position of servitude which demands in many respects self-restraint and a sense of responsibility. One may deplore or welcome that. One thing is sure, it is inevitable. It means that the affected millions need a new philosophy which does not only influence their actions in their profession, but must have an effect on their entire personality.

B You simply mean that modern man must feel more strongly a member of the community than his parents and he is therefore more restricted ethically.

A That is exactly what I meant to say.

B But that is really nothing new. Man in the middle ages also lived much less as an individual than as a member of his church, his guild, or other enforced institution. We really have no reason to re-introduce them.

A It is true that never has society given so much freedom to the individual as has been the case in the sphere of European civilisation of the last hundred years. I believe that nothing would be a greater mistake than a return to the restriction of the personality in the Middle Ages.

Human progress would surely stop in its tracks if the individual were once more robbed of his freedom of choice of his general path, i.e. choice of profession, spouse and conviction.

B You believe in the progress of humanity?

A Of course I believe in the possibility as well as in the reality of general progress. I take the meaning of the word progress to be the same as in nature. There we talk of a development of the forms of life from the simpler or lower to the more complicated or higher as the progress in a directed motion which constantly moves the goal forward as soon as it is reached. The essential difference between civilised and biological progress lies, as I see it, in the many times greater velocity of the progressing motion and the incomparably greater mobility of the goal.

B These trains of thought of yours are in fact not new. However, there is another side to the process of economic concentration which runs opposite to that which you have mentioned. It is true that, as you have mentioned, thousands and thousands of people are pressed into serving which was foreign to them before. On the other hand, the same process lifts an admittedly much smaller number of people to positions of economic power never known before. One does not talk for nothing of "kings" in the field of economics who practically rule the fate of millions. Assuming that a comparatively small number of leaders of economy decide to increase the wages in one industry or on a price increase of raw material, this might affect the economy of the whole country, possibly of the whole world. The people concerned in making the decision exert therefore a power which as the attribute of an individual is unequalled, measured by former standards.

A What you say there does to a great extent correspond with the real world. It is a different question, though, as to whether this particular effect of a general development is unavoidable and altogether desirable. I would deny both. I believe it to be a moral demand which arises from the general idea of human society in the only possible form at the present time, that everyone whose decisions and actions change the essential conditions of the entire society must be responsible to the entire society for his decisions and actions.

B This demand, considered by itself, seems very plausible. To pursue the question, we would also have to consider its political and economic aspect. I would not presume to give a judgment on it just like that. Particularly as it has nothing to do with our original discussion.

A I am not really of the opinion that political and economic questions have nothing to do with philosophy. But maybe you could now come back to your fundamental objections to my approach to the ethical ideal. You mentioned them earlier on. You said that they had not yet been appreciated in our discussion.

Tenth Dialogue

In this last discussion B lines up his remaining argument having been forced to revise his original opinions again and again in the preceding dialogues. In the end, he tries to point out that as the discussion had led after all to arguments which are unprovable, it is a matter of faith to accept or reject the matter. I leave it to the reader to judge for himself.

The discussion is, to begin with, about the inner conflicts which B likes to present as characteristic of A's proposed interpretation of the totality of the ethical ideal. Later on, the question is about the relation between theoretical insight regarding ethical matters, and practical philosophy in which moral ideas can be disseminated. A having by now refuted most of B's objections, the discussion turns finally to A's opinion that normal man can only become bad in the ethical sense through the unfavourable influence of the environment.

After a short digression about the part that fear of death plays in religious arguments, the discussion finally turns once more to the ideal of a class-free society.

B The real reason why I am repelled by your concept of the ethical ideal is its uncertainty which really lies in the fact that it is founded on such a fluctuating complex as "the entirety of all natural impulses of the human heart". You have stressed yourself that, according to the circumstances in individual cases, the ethical discussion might quite possibly take place against the call of inner urges which are otherwise deemed higher and nobler. I do not quite see where the firm basis can be, without which no ethics can exist.

A It is unavoidable that every kind of ethics has to demand that, in individual cases, even strong inner urges be repressed. The urge to act in individual cases against urges commonly considered as ethically positive is not specifically characteristic for the concept of the ethical problem as I have formulated it either.

You yourself uttered earlier on the opinion that ethical conflicts are not avoidable and are part of the nature of ethics. However, ethical conflicts can hardly be solved in fact without the disregard of just such higher impulses.

B There is, though, a powerful difference in whether the sacrifice of inner urges of whatever kind they may be is made to a higher principle whose very nature has nothing to do with the urges in question, or to a principle that represents no more than the entirety of the selfsame urges. It is this difference which seems to me to make uncertain the ethical decision as you see it.

You say that ethical conflict is unavoidable in any system of ethics, but this conflict is usually the exception, whereas in your determination of the ethically correct action, the conflict between the component parts of the ethical principle is no exception but simply the rule.

A Maybe the inner conflicts are the rule in any kind of ethics provided the ethical analysis of the individual case is taken far enough. This is undoubtedly the case in Christian ethics, for instance.

B You are probably thinking of the form Christian ethics took in the hands of Jesuit casuistics. You are right in that case. Yet the example given to us by the Jesuits is not suited to increase one's confidence in a philosophy which bases the ethical decision in principle on the circumstances of the individual case. The Jesuits' practice based on the casuistic theory has in any case not helped to give Jesuit teaching a good name.

A The Jesuits got a bad name only because they equated the greater honour of God, proclaimed to be the be all and end all of all action, with the interests of the Catholic church, which were frequently very material. The opinion which I have represented can hardly lead to an analogous equation in which general ideal goals are replaced by more or less limited practical interests.

B I do not think this possibility is quite so far-fetched. The ethical demand requires, according to you, only an optimum realisation. The concept of optimum is, however, hardly distinguishable from the concept of the lesser evil. In fact you stress very much the ethical duty to participate actively in the realisation of comprehensive material changes in the living conditions of human society.

I grant you that your opinion would in no case lead to the execution of otherwise dishonourable actions for the benefit of the Catholic church of which the Jesuits have been accused with or without justification.

Yet, who can vouch that in the eyes of some follower of your opinion the realisation of the class-free society represents so high a purpose that any means, even if they were usually considered reprehensible, would be justified to achieve it? They would appear the lesser evil with reference to the optimum of your definition.

A Your question forgets one circumstance which has played a great part in our recent discussion. It is the importance which general and in particular ethical ideas have for the continued development of human civilised society. If you had thought of that you could not have come to the conclusion that anybody who acts against ideas somehow fundamental for the development of society can believe that such action can be of service to the progress of society. If he undertakes them nevertheless, he must hinder instead of help progress.

B All right, I admit that your opinions yield no sound reason for neglecting ideal values in favour of material goals.

That does not alter the fact, however, that the moral ideas which form the basis of your philosophy do not form a unit free from contradiction, but are a complex in which the various components are, so to say, at war with each other, and you see the moral sovereignty of the individual saved by his freedom to take sides in this fight.

A consequence of the tensions between the various components of the complex of moral ideas is that one may not act in agreement with separate ideas of the complex without occasionally coming into conflict with its other ideas.

Starting from the beginning that you have chosen there is probably no other way out of the dilemma but the definition of the ethical ideals as the optimum in which a certain concession is inherent. However, this allots to the concept of good right from the beginning the character of a compromise and a pliability which is hardly compatible with its purpose of providing an absolute and inequivocal measure for the actions of man. Starting from your opinion, it ought to be very difficult, if not impossible, to arrive at effectively unequivocal, moral prohibitions. They are the firm backbone without which no ethics can exist.

A I think you make a mistake in linking the demand to be clear and un-equivocal with the demand to be absolute. I would like to draw on physics for an example. The concepts of above and below are clear and unequivocal, yet they imply no absolute direction as we well know since man first succeeded in sailing around the world. The tendency to look for absolute values is, in my opinion, one of the most dangerous for the seeker after truth no matter whether his subject is science, philosophy or sociology. The field of validity of a proven statement may expand or decrease in the course of scientific progress as we know from experience. Under no circumstances may the scientist ignore newly recognised relationships which make former knowledge relative, for the sake of the desired simplicity of the results.

B That may be true for research. Yet we were agreed that, where ethics are concerned, it is not only a question of pure knowledge but a matter of solving practical questions.

A I have something more to say about this practical side of the question which interests us both equally. I want to oppose firmly the negative interpretation of the ethical ideal which proclaims that the essence of all philosophy lies in the prohibitions it pronounces.

Would it not be better to measure the value of philosophy by the extent to which it is capable of inspiring man to positive achievements? Let us follow the natural dictates of our heart about what is good and what is bad. I think you will find that we do not judge our neighbours, nor do we measure the respect we pay them, by the sum of their large or small individual faults, but by their positive qualities as shown in their character and deeds. We are only inclined to condemn if the positive qualities seem to be lacking.

To judge a man and his actions as a whole means really no more than that we test the agreement of his deeds with the entire complex of ideas which direct the moral progress of society at the time. The measuring stick is of course not absolute, nor is it immutable historically considered, but it is as objective and as stable as may be expected at all.

B   I do not quarrel fundamentally with what you say about the necessity of an integral interpretation of moral matters. But do you think that the average man is capable of following intelligently the contest of moral ideas that form the background to the evolution of human society to such an extent as to be able to form a basis for practical decision in every individual case?

I admit that it is difficult to escape from the logic of the exposition of your thoughts, but do they not lead to a philosophy which can only be understood and used by a small number of educated elect in the innermost nature? After all, a philosophy which claims the right to general recognition ought not to have an esoteric character but ought to be capable of giving moral direction to the community in its widest sense. The large mass of humanity needs, in my opinion, firm moral principles which are easily understood. Material goals take their place all too easily when they are missing in the consciousness of the community. It may even be a favoured case in which the material goal, for which the ideals have been sacrificed, has a general, social character and does not simply result in the most common egoism.

A   Do you really think that the ethical convictions founded in mysticism and religion, which you indicated at the beginning of our discussion, stand a better chance of being brought close enough to avoid misunderstandings among the masses who, in your opinion, have little understanding?

B   To begin with, I would like to say to this that the ethical points of view which I mentioned at the beginning of our discussion have the character of questions rather than of answers. I have never believed that the form in which I was able to state them to you has ever constituted a fundamentally satisfactory solution of ethical questions. It was much less a solution suitable for moral direction to the community.

119

A Which is the way that you propose to take in order to arrive at a philosophy which is equal to this demand, or can you not see such a way?

B Confronted with the necessity of moral influence on the masses there may be no other way than to fall back onto the old recipe of using simplified and coarser formulae, even if they do not bear closer scrutiny. I know that this is hardly compatible with your principles. However, we must, in the end, console ourselves with the ancient wisdom that the world will be deceived and must occasionally be deceived to avoid greater damage.

A Do not take it ill if I point out to you that you use, yourself, the principle of the lesser evil to decide a moral question, for you must admit that the search for the most appropriate methods to influence morally the community is of a very moral character.

B I am not offended and agree that logic is once more on your side. But how are you going to meet my objection about the esoteric character of your opinions? I presume that you also are of the opinion that to-day it is not a question of a philosophy for the few but of a solution of urgent moral questions for all.

A Certainly. I think that your opinion that the masses have only a small capacity for higher ideal is absolutely wrong. It is therefore my opinion that it is a mistake to imagine that it is necessary to deceive the community in moral matters in order to avoid greater damage. The consequences, particularly in moral respects, could be only dangerous.

B Do you mean that, for instance, the problems of the theory of cognition, which occupied us in our first discussion, could be understood by the general mass without further ado?

A Well, not of course without effort. The theory of cognition is, after all, a branch of philosophy. As we have seen earlier, it must therefore occupy itself with the evaluation of the results of certain specialised sciences. That means that everyone wishing to pursue and understand the theory of cognition must be informed on the specialised results. As things are to-day it is furthermore impossible to pursue the theory of cognition to advantage without having come to grips with the well-known declarations of the idealistic school. That makes the subject more complicated and more difficult to understand than it really has to be according to its nature. But I do not really understand why you bring up the question about general plausibility of the theory of cognition at this moment.

B Well, we have disputed for a long time without having come to a complete agreement. That seems to prove to me that the subject of moral theory is even more complicated than that of the theory of cognition, certainly not simpler. And so it seems to me that your opinions are not suitable to make the problems which arise out of ethics more easily approachable.

A Possibly theory of cognition and moral theory are equally simple or equally complicated. Nevertheless one can surely arrive at correct factual knowledge without having studied and understood the theory of cognition in abstract. I think the same is valid in the field of ethics. Although the moral theory is difficult we know by experience that there is no difficulty in applying it correctly and there is no difficulty in acting in practice according to ethical ideas.

B But there lies the very objection to your definition of ethically correct actions. This definition demands of the participant as a condition for every ethic decision theoretical insight, which is to call for the non-existent.

A In that case, you have misunderstood me. No more is needed for the ethical decision of an actual case than to recognise in an imagined practical action certain general characteristics of the complex of ideas determining the ethical ideal. That presumes no theoretical insight nor the ability neither to name the characteristics in question. I believe we have discussed this point at length in an earlier dialogue. You quite agreed with my exposition that it is a great step from distinguishing concrete objects by abstract characteristics to the evaluation of the characteristics by means of language which would be necessary to name these characteristics. I think I had convinced you in the erstwhile discussion that the bird chooses the material for building its nest according to certain abstract characteristics. These determine the suitability for building the nest, and compose in their entirety the idea of the nest material which is inherited by the bird without having the ability of analysing the idea abstractly. You agreed with me that the difficulty of abstract thought which is the basis of science and also necessary in moral theory lies always in the necessity of judging abstract characteristics with the aid of usually equally abstract concepts. This is a difficulty particularly great when the observation of the characteristics to be determined demands that other, normally much more striking characteristics of the objects under observation must be overlooked, as happens so often in science. To be able to act ethically correctly neither is necessary, neither the abstract evaluation of the characteristics which make an action either good or bad in the ethical sense nor the suppression of the characteristics which are normally particularly impressive. The much-maligned concept of the optimum presupposes an integral manner of observation which does not allow any characteristic to be overlooked if it is important for setting into motion the course of action requiring an ethical decision. If you think that man is not able to recognise common characteristics in actual reality without first analysing these characteristics in the abstract, you obviously deny the human brain a fundamental quality which even higher animals possess.

B The very example of the bird building a nest that you have just given seems to me clearly to indicate that the complex of characteristics for human actions involved in moral ideas is something quite different from the characteristics of physical objects which release animal instincts. The bird can recognise the materials useful for building the nest without having and using higher abstract mental qualities simply because, according to your own convincing explanation, it is only a question of characteristics of a concrete nature which require for their recognition just a simple combination of sensations. The abstract character of the recognisable characteristics is the result of the abstract nature of the physical laws according to which all sensations are accomplished.

The characteristics which make an action good or bad, on the other hand, certainly do not have such purely sensuous qualities. I know I have myself suggested the use of the word idea also for complexes of sensuously given qualities of material objects. I think, nevertheless, that such ideas belong fundamentally to a different category than for instance the moral ideas. The latter presuppose, after all, a higher spiritual ability for their conception. Pursuance of your own ideas forces the assumption that higher spiritual activity includes undoubtedly also the analytical evaluation of the separate components of the entire complex of moral ideas. Without such an analysis it would be impossible to differentiate between the redundant parts of ideas hindering the progress of society and the progressive parts which are, according to you, the only ones to determine moral action.

The bird is of course incapable of an analogous analysis of which it has no need because the complex of sensuous characteristics making the idea of the nest material does not contain such inner conflicts.

A Moral ideas are a product of civilisation and cannot be conceived without the material and spiritual qualification which are the content of civilisation. In that respect I agree with you in ascribing to them a "higher" character. Yet I must contradict your assumption that they represent ideas fundamentally different from the ideas which guide the actions of animals. I hope to convince you when we come to discuss the nature of art that precisely those moral ideas may have a very close connection with ideas which can be defined by a complex of sense characteristics of concrete objects.

Also you make a mistake if you think that the bird is not confronted with a dilemma when it collects material for the nest suitable according to the idea of the nest. You must remember that we have discussed that conflicts must arise as soon as the instincts of animals are aroused in reality. The same is of course valid for the instincts belonging to nest building.

No material that the bird finds in nature has all the characteristics of an ideal case. Yet the bird will choose it provided it approaches what is the optimum under the given circumstances. The bird is repelled by the lack of some ideal characteristics. It is attracted by the presence of others. In the end, it is the integral over attracting and repelling impulses which are going to decide the behaviour of the bird. The carrier of the psychical processes does not have to investigate every one of the attractive or repulsive psychological moments involved to form the integral over them. I think that similar processes occur regularly in order to achieve the formation of man's will and without the analytical activity seated in the human brain which recognises every real characteristic active in motivating the action.

B So you think that the psychological process involved in an ethical decision takes place essentially in the unconscious. That is really exactly what I say.

A I have no objection to that statement provided you call unconscious all those moments and components of psychical processes which are not examined by the carrier at the time. I must, however, decline to connect another meaning with the word unconscious.

B Let us perhaps discuss the nature of the unconscious later on. First, I must say that I cannot see at all how unconscious psychical processes can be substituted for an historical investigation necessary to achieve an insight as to which of the components of the fund of ideas of the society is advantageous for the progress of the latter and which is disadvantageous. According to your opinion, no correct ethical decision can be made without such insight.

Apart from that it seems to me that the opinion of the actual ethical decision being made unconsciously is a contradiction of your opinion of the moral ideas as the ideas of civilisation. In a former talk you stressed the great importance of language for the assimilation of ideas which govern various members of the society at some time or other as well as for the further development of these ideas. How can the moral ideas take place in the development of civilisation when they are excluded from the analytical examination necessary for their transmission by language?

A Let me go into your last objection first. I have never said that objective analysis is entirely inapplicable to moral ideas. I have no wish to dispute that their transmission in analytic form plays a prominent part in the development of civilised society. But one must not overestimate this part. The ethical ideal that is significant in its entirety at some time for a group in the same social situation is always of so complex a structure that it can never be really grasped completely.

In fact, it can only achieve its practical historic importance because means of communication in existence are independent of such an analytical treatment. Art, for instance, is such a means of communication. But the most important medium is one that is not at all intellectual nor is it at all esoteric. It is the example everybody sets for his contemporaries by his own conduct of life.

On this occasion, I would like to point out a circumstance which is, in my opinion, of decisive importance for the understanding of all moral problems. It is this. Isolated moral ideas have in practice no significance for either the individual or society as a whole, but only in context with an entire complex of ideas in which the connections are, as a rule, not purely logical but quite as much practical.

The transmission by example of ideas in common by the way with the artistic statement has the great advantage that in this way no isolated idea is ever transmitted, but only entire complexes. The case of the practical example is the transmission of the entire complex of ideas relating to the model behaviour.

B I have my own opinions about art and its moral effectiveness. We might talk about that later. First of all, however, I must contradict your opinion about the part played by the practical example of the transmission of the ethical ideal. If the good example were as effective as you believe, the bad example which obviously exists also ought to be equally effective on the whole. There is no reason why the over-all influence of the good examples should outweigh the over-all influence of the bad examples. This would be necessary in order to produce the moral progress of humanity in which you also believe, I take it.

A The good example is nothing but the demonstration of a form of ideas appropriate to the conditions of the time. They are in any case contained potentially in every human breast from the start. They have only to be excited in order to unfold their complete effectiveness. The observer of a foreign moral example experiences attraction or repulsion in the same way as with respect to the perception of his own action. Should repulsion outweigh attraction, he will feel the given example not to be good but bad and will therefore not be inclined to follow it. Only this elementary method is necessary in order to decide between moral ideas serving the progress of society and those hindering it. The decision does not demand a historical analysis of social evolution as you considered necessary. After all, a moral idea which hinders the progress in the battle of ideas does not hinder and therefore become injurious because it had significance in the past. No, it only does so once it cannot be realised in practice without offending against inner urges in the human breast which have significance or which have acquired significance in the course of moral social evolution, and which must now be absolutely satisfied for the realisation of the moral optimum. Such inner urges can, of course, be experienced, even in a particularly immediate and original manner, by persons who do not think of a reasonable analysis of these urges. Indeed, they may not be able to do so.

Bad examples are indeed imitated at times even by very large numbers. We have already discussed the reasons for this and have found that they are concerned with the tendency of the entire cultural complexes of ideas to lag behind for biological and cultural reasons.

B   I think our discussion about the ethical problem has reached a point where to continue seems senseless because our differences of opinion no longer concern questions capable of proof but of belief. Your opinions are certainly consistent in themselves. I really know of no pertinent rational argument to throw weight into the scales against them. That I am nevertheless not willing to follow you is above all the fault of the optimism which is fundamentally the basis of your convictions and which is incapable of proof in the final analysis. You simply start with the fundamental assumption that man, according to his true and original nature, taken as a whole, is absolutely good and does not need correction from outside or, by interference from a higher sphere, need to become worthy of positive ethical evaluation.

You are probably to be envied for this conviction of yours. I would say it is essential if one undertakes, like you, to base the ethical ideal on the entirety of all impulses active inside man. However, I do not think I can quite bring myself to do that just yet.

A   It is indeed my conviction that every healthy man is naturally good. I mean that an optimum possible satisfaction of all his original impulses exists for him. He has only to make the realisation of these impulses his supreme guiding star in order to be instrumental to the progress of human society and to become a member of society worthy of respect and recognition.

I cannot, however, endorse your opinion that this conviction is only a matter of belief and cannot be proved in principle.

On the contrary, it seems to me that social experience shows clearly that moral aberrations, apart from organic illness in the carrier, are always connected with specific social and material environmental influences of historical origin, without which they could not be produced.

B   I must confess that I feel a certain inner resistance against accepting your opinion for another reason. We have mentioned it briefly, by the way, in our very first discussion. As you know, I am fundamentally a sceptic where the evaluation of concrete conditions is concerned. Yet I am afraid, possibly too much occasionally, that I am subject to misconceptions in this respect. That is why I find it difficult, on the other hand, to deny the possibility of the existence of higher phenomena not connected with nature. I would have to do so if I were to agree with you unconditionally.

A I cannot, strictly speaking, understand your objection. The need for the assumption of supernatural powers exists in fact only for as long as there are reasons to think it hopeless to be able to explain the world through natural phenomena.

However, you are yourself a scientist. At the present state of scientific knowledge, and in face of its continual progress, you must agree with me that it would be frivolous to claim of any yet unexplained phenomena whatsoever that the answer to the question it poses is impossible without the assumption of the supernatural.

B I have not yet given you one essential reason why I cannot bring myself to deny absolutely every religious idea. It is actually not rational, but rather intuitive, and you may think it a ridiculous weakness. However, I do not think I am the only one subject to it. It is the disinclination to admit that everything ends with death. Do you understand me? I do not demand, like Kant, that a higher power should reward me after death for the good deeds which brought me no gain in life. I think I have left you in no doubt that to my mind this thought is morally inferior. I have simply an elementary horror of the thought that when my heart stands still and my breath stops that all that has inspired me should end in nothing. And that is the conclusion one cannot escape if one lets oneself be guided only by scientific knowledge.

A Philosophy is a science. It is not the task of science to console but to make possible the progressive recognition of truth. Without it mankind could not pursue its way, which is after all in a forward direction.

However, I think that the horror of death you spoke of is not quite as elementary as you think. It is founded on the incorrect concept of the reality of human life. The mistake is to see man as an individual and nothing more. Let us assume that I have learnt to conceive my life and activity only in relation to myself, as is doubtlessly the case for a great number of the members of our generation. In that case, death must indeed appear as the descent into the abyss which robs of all meaning everything of importance to me. This concept of one's own life is, however, the very opposite to truth. Our preceding discussions can have left no doubt that no man who deserves the name man can live in practice other than as a member of the big human society as well as one of many subdivisions of society. Without them his life would be without the meaning which makes his life human.

With the death of a human being something dies which has never existed except as part of a whole which continues to exist.

We have seen, furthermore, that in man's breast the undeniable dominating role is played by fundamentally extrovert impulses which in their entirety compose the impulse to act. Anyway, they play a far greater part than in any other living being. Anyone for whom his own person is the centre of all interest would with this attitude certainly fail his call to humanity. He would unavoidably disgrace mankind.

However, anyone who has understood these circumstances correctly will consider his person as a tool for the achievement of goals which put the tool itself completely in the shade. He will consider the depreciation of the tool and its final unavoidable end in no way a reason for despair. More important than the plough is the furrow that it has made which receives the seed and nourishes the fruit. The plough has perished, yet the seed produces other seed and gives meaning to all ploughs which have ever ploughed the ground.

Do not give me the reply that only a few but not the millions are capable of achieving reactions which bear fruit in the development of the civilisation of mankind.

It is precisely by the moral influence, by the example of his own life, as we have mentioned recently, that everyone ploughs a furrow which is really irradicable, and thus he adds his contribution to the creation of ideas according to which future generations form themselves.

B I will gladly admit that there is a certain consolation in this when one comes to think of death provided one has really absorbed these thoughts and is conscious of having acted accordingly. Notwithstanding that you, as a philosopher, have rejected in principle the intention to console.

On the other hand, it seems to me that the principle you have just uttered contains also some quite dangerous moments. You mentioned that man must first and foremost serve as a tool for the realisation of general goals which are independent of the individual and his individual existence. There is nothing to object to in this concept as long as the individual is guided by it only with respect to the conduct of his own life. What happens, however, if he starts to take this point of view when he considers others whose fate may be in his hand? It could, in my opinion, lead to extremely objectionable consequences, even when we assume the most favourable case that the goals for which man is to be misused as a blind tool are really of the ideal kind.

A I would think that only people with individualistic opinions can be tempted to use their contemporaries as blind tools to realise goals which they do not want. Persons who have overcome these concepts must know that such a procedure contradicts the natural ideal of human society — at any rate, the ideal of the class-free society, the only one which can still be valid for us. It is fundamental that in the class-free society everyone who is concerned in the ideal and material maintenance and development of civilisation must enjoy equal moral rights. They must in no way be robbed of the possibility of serving their volition, and they must be conscious of that fact. This excludes the possibility that one section of society uses another section as mere blind tools.

It is a very different matter, however, for someone to manage by his own example to convert others into putting their own life into the service of higher general goals. He does a great service not only to society but to each separate individual. In this way, he helps the latter to follow his true human calling.

B You say that in the class-free society it is not permissible that one individual can dispose of another. It seems to me that applies also to the class society, at least with respect to the relations of members of one and the same class.

A I dare say you are right by and large. Nevertheless, this question has hardly any actual interest for us. It is my opinion that the class society is dead, if not in fact, yet so in the consciousness of any part of present mankind of somewhat progressive thought. From the point of view of morals it deserves therefore no more than historical interest.

B There I agree with you!

PRINTED IN GERMANY

Volksdruckerei Sonneberg, Betriebsteil Hildburghausen V 9 1